The World of Witold Gombrowicz, 1904–1969

The World of
WITOLD GOMBROWICZ
1904–1969

VINCENT GIROUD

Catalog of a centenary exhibition at the Beinecke Rare Book & Manuscript Library, Yale University

NEW HAVEN, CONNECTICUT, 2004
DISTRIBUTED BY UNIVERSITY PRESS OF NEW ENGLAND

This publication accompanies the exhibition of the same name held at the Beinecke Rare Book & Manuscript Library, Yale University, New Haven, Connecticut, October 22 through December 2004.

Cover: Photograph by Hanne Garthe

LIBRARY OF CONGRESS CATALOGING-IN-PUBLICATION DATA

Beinecke Rare Book and Manuscript Library.
The world of Witold Gombrowicz 1904–1969 : catalog of a centenary exhibition at the Beinecke Rare Book & Manuscript Library, Yale University / Vincent Giroud. — 1st ed.
p. cm.
Exhibition, consisting almost entirely of materials from the Witold Gombrowicz Archive in the Beinecke Library, held Oct. 22–Dec. 2004.
Includes bibliographical references.
ISBN 0-8457-3158-0 (alk. paper)
1. Gombrowicz, Witold—Exhibitions. 2. Gombrowicz, Witold—Archives—Exhibitions. 3. Beinecke Rare Book and Manuscript Library—Exhibitions. I. Giroud, Vincent. II. Title.

PG7158.G6692B45 2004
891.8'5373—dc22

2004022587

Page 21: Excerpt from *Ferdydurke*, translated by Danuta Borchardt (New Haven and London: Yale University Press, 2000), by permission of Yale University Press.

Page 37: Excerpt from *Diary. Volume 2, 1957–1961*. Edited by Jan Kott. Translated by Lillian Vallee (Evanston: Northwestern University Press, 1989), by permission of Northwestern University Press.

Page 63: Excerpt from *Operetta*, translated by Louis Iribarne (London: Calder and Boyars, 1971), by permission of Marion Boyars Publishers.

PHOTOGRAPH CREDITS

Rita Gombrowicz took or collected many of the photographs in the exhibition and catalog; those on pages 26, 32, and 57 (top) are attributed to her
Page 46: Miguel Grinberg, Collection Rita Gombrowicz
Page 58 (top); page 65 (top): Photo Leprince, Collection Rita Gombrowicz
Page 60; page 65 (middle): Bohdan Paczowski, Collection Rita Gombrowicz
Page 65 (lower): Oswald Malura, Collection Rita Gombrowicz
Page 66: Hanne Garthe, Collection Rita Gombrowicz

COLOPHON

Edited by Christa Sammons and James Mooney

Printed by Herlin Press • Bound by Acme Bookbinding Company

Design and Typography by Howard I. Gralla

FOR RITA GOMBROWICZ

INTRODUCTION

The greatest prose writer of twentieth-century Polish letters, Witold Gombrowicz is also recognized as a figure whose literary standing is comparable to Proust, Joyce, Kafka, Musil, or Beckett. Yet his reputation in the United States and the English-speaking world has never been equal to his renown in continental Europe or in Latin America. In a letter to an American publisher preserved in his archive at the Beinecke Library, he writes that he hoped to be read in America some day, at least by the élite. Yet Gombrowicz is no élitist writer. His first novel, *Ferdydurke*, its moral and philosophical implications notwithstanding, is as funny as Molière or Lewis Carroll. His three plays—*Yvonne, princess of Burgundy, The marriage,* and *Operetta*—have been successfully produced in many countries and have acquired a permanent place in the repertory. His *Diary*, in more than 1,200 pages, is an account, in turn moving and humorous, of his experience of exile, a document on the intellectual polemics of the post–World War II period, and a philosophical journal in the manner of Montaigne. Reading Gombrowicz, or attending a performance of one of his plays, is an exhilarating and profoundly liberating experience. This remains the case today as it was for the young Poles who discovered his work at the height of the Communist period. He is, as Józef Czapski has pointed out, a great debunker of all false reputations and false values. In this and other respects, such as the philosophical underpinnings of much of his writing, it is appropriate, as Wojciech Karpinski has suggested recently, to see in him a modern Nietzsche.

Gombrowicz was born a century ago, an anniversary observed in the spring of 2004 in Poland and other countries of Europe. The Yale commemoration is part of the "Gombrowicz Autumn" on the East Coast and in other parts of the United States, which will feature performances of his plays, screenings of film adaptations of his works, photographic exhibitions, and a variety of other public programs, as well as publications by and about him, including some of his work available in English for the first time. The presence in the Beinecke Library of the Gombrowicz Archive, next to the papers of several fellow Polish émigré writers, was enough to justify that Yale play a major part in this celebration. In conjunction with this exhibition, an international symposium on Gombrowicz, sponsored jointly by the Beinecke Library, the Department of Slavic Languages and Literatures, and Yale

University Press, will gather scholars, writers, and translators from Argentina, France, Poland, and the United States. A special issue of *Theater*, the magazine published under the auspices of the Yale School of Drama, will be devoted to Gombrowicz, while the stage adaptation of *Ferdydurke* by the Teatr Provisorium Company (made possible through a generous gift from Piotr and Judy Chomczynski) will be presented at the University Theater.

For this collaborative effort, thanks are due above all to Pawel Potoroczyn, director of the Polish Cultural Institute in New York. An enthusiastic supporter of this initiative, he was also a major partner in it, as well as the coordinator of the many other events marking the Gombrowicz Autumn in America.

Barbara Shailor, former director of the Beinecke Library, gave her wholehearted support to this project, a support generously confirmed by her successor, Frank M. Turner, John Hay Whitney Professor of History. Much gratitude is also due to Harvey Goldblatt, chair of the Department of Slavic Languages and Literatures; Tomas Venclova, professor of Slavic Languages and Literatures; Jonathan Brent, senior editor at Yale University Press; and Thomas Sellar, assistant professor in the Yale School of Drama and editor of *Theater*.

While the exhibition is drawn almost entirely from the Witold Gombrowicz Archive in the Beinecke Library, the Sterling Memorial Library kindly lent two items, one of them from its Map Collection, whose curator, Frederick Musto, deserves warm thanks for this help. The preparation of this exhibition and catalog coincided with the cataloging of the Gombrowicz Archive. This was the work of Monika Talar, archivist at the State Archive in Wroclaw and the recipient of the Witold Gombrowicz Internship created for that purpose at the Beinecke's initiative in partnership with the Polish Cultural Institute and with the active support of the Cultural Services of the American Embassy in Warsaw, where Iza Szarek particularly deserves our thanks. My own thanks go to Monika Talar for her generous and knowledgeable assistance.

The Yale Gombrowicz commemoration owes a great deal to contacts over the years with Gombrowicz scholars, especially from Poland, who have visited New Haven to work on the archive. Among them, I am particularly indebted to Jerzy Jarzebski, currently the dean of Gombrowicz studies, whose wonderfully titled

1982 study *Playing the Gombrowicz Game* is still waiting to be translated, for inviting me to participate in the international conference he organized at the Jagellonian University in Cracow in March 2004. This exceptional gathering—which by the account of its president was the largest academic conference held at the university—was an opportunity for useful exchanges with Gombrowicz scholars. Special thanks must be conveyed, in particular, to Piotr Millati and Klementyna Suchanow, both recipients of Beinecke visiting fellowships in 2003–04, to Carlos Barinaga, and, in this country, to Allen Kuharski.

Wojciech Karpinski, as always, was an invaluable source of inspiration, in conversation and through his writings on the authors of the Gombrowicz generation—books he describes, in a phrase first adapted by Mickiewicz after Schiller, as "highway robbers." For permissions to reproduce some of the illustrations of this catalog, thanks are due to Hanne Garthe, Miguel Grinberg, and Bohdan Paczowski. Danuta Borchardt and Bill Johnston kindly answered queries about their translations of works by Gombrowicz. Crucial help was provided at all stages of this project by Timothy Young, assistant curator of modern books and manuscripts, who, in particular, oversaw the preparation of an online Polish version of the exhibition, the scanning of illustrations, and the mounting of its audiovisual component. It is fair to say that the exhibition could not have taken place without him. As always, Christa Sammons and James Mooney were the expert text editors and Howard Gralla performed wonders in meeting seemingly impossible deadlines with elegance and efficiency.

Alexander Schenker, professor emeritus of Slavic Languages and Literatures, whose kind mentoring has guided the growth of Yale's modern Polish collections over the past seventeen years, was the first reader of this catalog and gave invaluable advice. All remaining errors and infelicities are mine.

The exhibition and catalog are dedicated to Rita Gombrowicz, whose work on behalf of her husband's oeuvre has earned her the admiration and loyalty of researchers and readers. Having herself drawn from the archive for her two irreplaceable biographical volumes, she chose Yale as its home, thereby making it accessible to scholars worldwide. This dedication is a small token of our gratitude and our affection.

Vincent Giroud

CHAPTER ONE *Maloszyce to Ferdydurke, 1904–39*

The Gombrowicz house in Maloszyce.

Gombrowicz with his mother, his sister, and his aunt at Bodzechów in 1913.

Witold Marian Gombrowicz was born on 4 August 1904 at Maloszyce, the family property in the Opatow district of the province of Sandomierz, in Little Poland, about 120 miles south of Warsaw. That part of Poland was then under Russian domination, while the north belonged to Germany and the south, including Cracow, was part of the Austro-Hungarian Empire. Of Lithuanian gentry stock, the Gombrowicz family had been forced to sell its vast estates following the imprisonment and exile of Witold's grandfather, implicated in the 1863 nationalist uprising. Gombrowicz's father, Jan Onufry (1868–1933), devoted himself successfully to the administration of his estates. In addition to Maloszyce, these included Jakubowice, also situated in Malopolska, and, on his wife's side, Bodzechów, near the industrial city of Ostrowiec. Gombrowicz's mother, Marcelina Antonina Kotkowska, came from a prosperous, aristocratic background with Radziwill connections. Her father had discovered and mined dolomite and brownstone quarries in the mountains near Doly, which provided building material for the Bristol Hotel and the Potocki Mansion (now the ministry of culture) in Warsaw. Reminiscing about his parents years later, Gombrowicz characterized his father with the words correctness, practical sense, propriety, order. The words he used to describe his mother, several of whose relatives had sunk into madness, were exaltation, nervousness, decadence, anarchy, dependency, aestheticism. He also noted that her artistic sensibility, to which he attributed his own creativity, was matched by self-delusion. To that side of her personality, Gombrowicz ascribed his attraction to the irrational and the nonsensical and his irrepressible taste for paradox and provocation.

Gombrowicz also retained from his mother's side a lifelong passion for genealogy and aristocratic precedence (his first literary achievement, in his late teens, was a compilation on the "illustrissima familia Gombrowici"). This Proust-like trait, evidenced in Gombrowicz's later passion for the memoirs of the Duc de Saint-Simon and by several handwritten or self-typed family trees in his archive, remained with him in the most difficult moments of his life as an exile. While driving genuine aristocrats like the painter Józef Czapski to evident exasperation, it found a sympathetic echo in his younger friend Konstanty (Constantin) Jelenski, the greatest champion of Gombrowicz's work in the 1950s and 1960s, who also had aristocratic connections.

Gombrowicz was the youngest child of Jan Onufry and Antonina Gombrowicz. Even after being separated from his siblings after 1939, he remained close to them, as revealed by his surviving correspondence with his elder brothers Janusz (1894–1968) and Jerzy (1895–1971) and his sister Irena (1899–1961), who, like him, was to die of asthma.

The revolutionary events of 1905 in Russia had repercussions in Poland. At Bodzechów, where the Gombrowicz family had settled in that year, Jan Onufry was a industrialist known for his progressive social tendencies and his opposition to Tsarist policies. In 1908 he was arrested and jailed for a short while in Radom. After a three-year trial, he was sentenced to a two-year imprisonment. Forced to relinquish his responsibilities in the management of Bodzechów, he moved his family to Warsaw and began to serve his term until his pardon by the tsar.

By his own account, both in his autobiographical writings and in the unfinished play *History*, the young Gombrowicz reacted to this enlightened and privileged background in his own discreetly radical way by a skeptical view of upper-class values and a fascination with the lower estate. After receiving private tutoring in French and German, he was sent, in 1915, to the Catholic high school known as Wielopolski or St. Stanislas Kostka, attended by children of the best families. It left him with mostly painful memories.

While Gombrowicz was at school, the First World War was tearing apart an already divided Poland: the socialist Józef Pilsudski, the future leader of independent Poland, fought on the Austro-German side until the summer of 1917, whereas Roman Dmowski, the leader of the nationalist right, joined the Russian war effort. Gombrowicz's experience of the war, which he witnessed at Maloszyce, close to what was then the Austrian border, made him a lifelong internationalist and pacifist, an evolution that paralleled his individualism and atheism.

After receiving his high school diploma in 1922 (despite failing grades in Latin, algebra, and trigonometry), Gombrowicz, to the disappointment of his father who had hoped he would follow his career in industry, enlisted, without much enthusiasm, as a law student at the University of Warsaw. Around that time, he experienced the first symptoms of pulmonary disease, for which, in keeping with the customs of the times, he was sent at

Gombrowicz (lower right) and his siblings at Potoczek in 1928.

regular intervals to recover in the mountain resort of Zakopane, to the south of Cracow. There he wrote a novel, which he later destroyed. His other literary efforts, which he described as attempts to write deliberately "bad," sentimental fiction, met the same fate. He paid regular visits to his brother Jerzy, now married to the descendant of a friend of Chopin's and living in his estate of Wsola, near Radom. There Gombrowicz had his first love affair, with a young woman living in the vicinity. This liaison lasted for a few years, during which he resisted his family's efforts to marry him to a countess.

Having taken his law degree, Gombrowicz spent the year 1928–29 in France. He first studied at the Institut d'études internationales in Paris and then moved to the Mediterranean coast near the Pyrénées mountains. There, by his own admission, he was close to a group of young men involved in the white slave trade. Only the protection of a priest saved him from serious trouble with the law.

On his return to Warsaw, Gombrowicz worked as clerk to the judge (a relative) who headed the Warsaw city tribunal. "I was incapable of telling the judges from the murderers," he later commented, "and it was with the latter that I shook hands." His legal career ended shortly afterwards, when his employment as a clerk to an attorney in Radom was blocked by the conservative bar association of the city, alarmed by his growing reputation of dandyism and flippancy.

By then, Gombrowicz had begun to associate with literary circles in the Polish capital and had written the short stories collected in the volume the publisher Rój issued in 1933 under the title *Pamietnik z okresu dorjrzewania* (*Memories of the time of immaturity*). The publication was financed by his father.

Memories of the time of immaturity comprises seven stories: "Lawyer Kraykowski's dancer" (dated 1926), "Memoirs of Stefan Czarniecki" (1926), "A premeditated crime" (1928), "Dinner at Countess Pavahoke's" (1928), "Virginity" (1928), "Adventures" (1930; the Polish title is "Five minutes before going to sleep"), and "The events on the Banbury" (1932). Unpublished in English until 2004, these tales are as striking today as they must have seemed at the time of their first appearance. Their tone and subject matter were characterized by their author as "fantastic, eccentric, and bizarre" as well as "morbid, revolting, repugnant": the quasi-erotic obsession of a young man with a fashionable lawyer about town; the existential malaise of a half-Jewish boy (originally called Jakob, he was renamed Stefan by Gombrowicz after the war) and its consequences on his adult life; a lawyer turned detective who, through psychological blackmail, manages to convince a bereaved son that he murdered his father; a luncheon given by a fashionable hostess that turns out to be a cannibalistic ritual; the carnal fantasies of a young woman whose fiancé venerates sexual purity; a fantastic, Swiftian tale set in exotic settings; and an equally fantastic, disturbing ocean voyage on a schooner bound for South America. Gombrowicz excluded from the volume the story "On the kitchen steps," dated 1929, a tale of erotic fantasies about maids and cooks, published only in 1937 in the journal *Skamander.*

Gombrowicz later blamed his choice of title for the indifference, even derision that greeted *Memories of the time of immaturity*. There was, to be sure, an enthusiastic review by Tadeusz Breza, who compared Gombrowicz to Edgar Allan Poe and Raymond Roussel. Otherwise, the ironic, parodistic quality of the stories, their emphasis on cruelty, their unusual brand of modernism, which owed nothing to Kafka or Joyce (whom Gombrowicz had not read) nor even to Freud (whom he claimed he had barely heard about at the time) were altogether lost on the reviewers, most of whom harped on the author's self-proclaimed immaturity.

Yet the book was noticed by the literary intelligentsia in Warsaw, and Gombrowicz found himself the object of the attention of the

Polish intellectual élite. The Warsaw literary scene at the time was dominated by the group of poets known as Skamander. Its chief members were Kazimierz Wierzynski (1894–1969), Julian Tuwim (1894–1953), Jaroslaw Iwaszkiewicz (1894–1980), Antoni Slonimski (1895–1976), Stanislaw Balinski (1898–1984), and Jan Lechón (1899–1956). Balinski and Iwaszkiewicz both made disparaging comments on *Memories from the time of immaturity*, the latter pronouncing the stories "too literary." Gombrowicz started frequenting the Ziemianska Café, where the Skamandrists had their table, but he kept his distance from them, even though he started contributing to *Skamander* as well as to another journal, *Wiadomosci literackie*, which they dominated. He began, instead, to attract his own coterie of younger friends and admirers, drawn to his studied eccentricity. By his own later account, supported by the testimonies of Czapski and Gustaw Herling-Grudzinski, who both met him at the time, the pre-war Gombrowicz, who was already well versed in philosophy, cultivated the persona of a latter-day sophist.

In December 1933, Jan Onufry Gombrowicz died suddenly of a cerebral hemorrhage. Witold inherited half of Maloszyce and acquired a share in other family-owned real estate.

Around the time of his father's death, Gombrowicz started writing his first play, *Iwona, ksieznicka Burgunda* (*Yvonne, princess of Burgundy*), which, though completed by 1935, was published only in 1938 in *Skamander*. The imaginary, burlesque Burgundy of *Iwona* is no more historical than the Poland of *Ubu Roi* ("The scene is in Poland, that is nowhere"). The dramaturgy of Gombrowicz's first play, in fact, bears some clear resemblance to Alfred Jarry's farce, while the cruelty of its theme is not unrelated to the stories of *Memories of the time of immaturity*. Philippe, the unmarried heir to the throne, encounters a girl, chaperoned by her two aunts, who is so aggressively unprepossessing ("awkward, apathetic, anemic, shy, nervous, and boring," in the playwright's words) that, after taunting her, he feels provoked into proposing to her, and presents her as his fiancée to the horrified court. Once at the court, Yvonne, while losing none of her ungainliness, becomes an "agent of decomposition." Although she remains silent throughout, opening her mouth only six times in the entire play, her mute presence acts as a constant reproach, forcing the queen to confess that she is addicted to writing awful, sentimental poetry, while Philippe is prompted, out of pure sadism, to flirt with a lady from the court in front of Yvonne.

In the end, a plot is engineered to get Yvonne to choke on a fish bone in the course of the wedding banquet. She dies and all becomes normal again.

Iwona, which seemed to respond to Artaud's call for a théâtre de la cruauté, while anticipating the plays by Beckett, Genet, and Ionesco by ten to fifteen years, found no theater director to produce it in the 1930s. It had to wait until 1957 for its first performance—a unique case in the annals of twentieth-century theater, especially considering the fact that it is now regarded as a modern classic.

In 1934, Gombrowicz made the acquaintance of Bruno Schulz, the artist and art teacher in the small town of Drohobycz, whose collection of short stories, *The cinnamon stores,* had just been published. The shy, withdrawn Schulz was the opposite of a literary establishment figure. He and Gombrowicz, his junior by ten years, bonded immediately. Despite aesthetic differences, Gombrowicz was never to deviate from his admiration and affection for his Jewish friend, who was shot by a Nazi soldier in a street of his home town in 1942. Through Schulz, Gombrowicz met the other writer he most esteemed in the pre-war generation, the playwright Ignacy Witkiewicz, born in 1885, who used the pen name Witkacy, and who was to kill himself the day the Soviet army invaded Poland in 1939. In Gombrowicz's view, Schulz and Witkiewicz, and by implication himself, unlike the writers of the Skamander group, had literary ambitions that transcended the strict confines of Poland to reach out to a wider, international audience—a claim which, at least in his and Schulz's case, has been validated by posterity.

The phrase "modern classic" applies even more to Gombrowicz's next work, *Ferdydurke.* The novel was written in 1935–36, in Warsaw, where Gombrowicz lived in a house, which is still standing, at no. 35 Chocimska Street, and while staying with his brother at Wsola, where his observations of the local gentry clearly provided fodder for the cruel satire of the final part, as Jerzy Gombrowicz has suggested.

The title *Ferdydurke,* a nonsense phrase (or name?) that Susan Sontag has likened to Lewis Carroll's *Jabberwocky,* was long considered an enigma, until a Polish scholar discovered its source in Sinclair Lewis's *Babbitt.* The American novelist, winner of the 1930 Nobel Prize for Literature, was then at the height of his

Portrait of Bruno Schulz by S. L. Witkiewicz (1935) and photograph of Schulz in 1934, from Jerzy Ficowski, ed., *Bruno Schulz Ksiega listów* (Cracow: Wydawnictwo Literackie, n.d.).

popularity and *Babbitt*, first published in 1922, was read all over the world. The quotation occurs at the start of the episode "Power and prosperity in public speaking," subtitled "A yarn told at the club": "Who do you think I ran into the other evening at the De Luxe Restaurant? Why, old Freddy Durkee, that used to be a dead or alive shipping clerk in my old place—Mr. Mouse-Man we used to laughingly call the dear fellow." Gombrowicz presumably appropriated the name, altering it only slightly, for its sheer phonetic, comical value. As for the lack of connection between the title and the novel, it was a mocking response to the critics who had pounced on his "immaturity" on account of the title he had given to his first book.

Told in the first person by a narrator who introduces himself as the 32-year-old author of a book entitled *Memoirs from the time of immaturity* (his name, however, is Joe Kowalski—a Polish equivalent of Smith or Jones), *Ferdydurke* is as strikingly original in its form as in its theme. Gombrowicz himself later commented that it was more a pamphlet than a novel. It could also be called an "anti-novel," in the tradition of Rabelais (to whom there is a direct reference in chapter 11) or *Tristam Shandy*, or even the Dickens of the *Pickwick Papers*, a book Gombrowicz admired enormously. As in *Don Quixote*, the narrative is interrupted, twice, by short stories unrelated to the plot: "The child runs deep in Filidor" and "The child runs deep in Filibert." Written in 1934, before Gombrowicz started *Ferdydurke* (the first appeared in 1935 in the *Gazeta Polska*), they are so detachable from the book that Gombrowicz later included them in the new edition of his short stories. They are both preceded by prefaces, the first of which reads like a manifesto.

A philosophical tale in the Voltairean sense, *Ferdydurke* has a memorable cast of characters: Professor Pimko, the "cultural philologue from Kraków," who in the opening chapter transforms the narrator into an adolescent and registers him as a pupil in Mr. Piórkowski's school; the students, from the idealist Syphon to the bully Kneadus, whose rough, oversexed manners conceal an attraction to farm boys (a trait not entirely devoid of autobiographical relevance); the engineer Youngblood and his wife, at whose house the narrator is a boarder; their daughter Zuta, whom Kowalski unsuccessfully courts; Kowalski's aunt, uncle, and cousins at the country château, where Kneadus falls in love with a farm boy and the whole social order is turned upside down in a carnival-like finale reminiscent of Rabelais or Jean Renoir's near-contemporary film *La règle du jeu*.

This joyfully subversive novel, which contains many of the themes Gombrowicz continued to explore in his later works, was published in October 1937 (with a 1938 imprint date) by Rój, the same house that had issued Gombrowicz's previous book. Gombrowicz paid for half of the printing costs.

The publication of *Ferdydurke* was greeted with indifference and incomprehension. There were enthusiastic reactions, such as the one by Herling-Grudzinski, but more typical was the one reported by Jelenski, many years later, in a letter to François Bondy. Jelenski's aunt, who knew Witold's sister as a fellow member of the board of the association of young Polish women landowners, gave a copy to her 16-year-old nephew with the comment: "You who read so much, tell me what you think of this unreadable book—it was written by Rena Gombrowicz's brother, she thinks he has lost his mind."

Schulz, who designed the cover of *Ferdydurke*, was also, to Gombrowicz's eternal gratitude, among the first to recognize in *Ferdydurke* a work of genius. In the spring of 1938, he gave a talk on a novel at the Writers' Union in Warsaw, which he published in the July–September numbers of *Skamander*. Late in his life, Gombrowicz continued to refer to Schulz's commentary as the most profound analysis of the work. Schulz stressed the book's striking originality from three points of view: its emphasis on the theme of immaturity; its central concept of form; and the fact that the novel itself creates its own form.

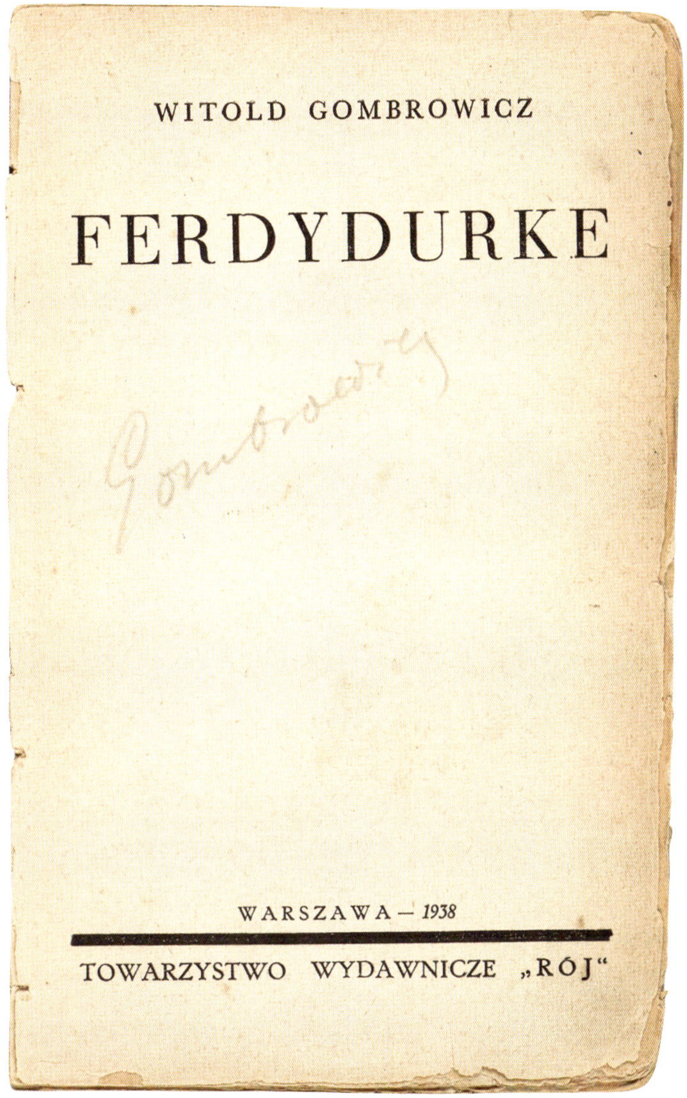

Ferdydurke was actually issued in 1937. From the library of Witold Gombrowicz.

Ferdydurke, Schulz argued, convincingly demonstrates that beneath our "official" selves, adult, rational, socialized, respectable, cultivated, there remain elements of immaturity, irrationality, anarchy, roguishness, which try to come to the surface and, when they do, expose the inauthenticity of established customs, manners, beliefs, ideologies, and culture. Gombrowicz described human beings as determined by what he calls "the form," or rather a multiplicity of forms, in other words, the ways in which we manifest ourselves and interact with each other: speech, ideas, actions and so forth. What we consider our truest, most authentic self is often, in fact, just a "mask" (the term used in *Ferdydurke* is "mug"). Far from arguing that we can actually free ourselves from the form, Gombrowicz suggests that we can strive for greater authenticity by at least coming to terms with our own immaturity rather than hiding it or disguising it. Schulz drew a perceptive analogy with Freud (an author Gombrowicz was somewhat familiar with by then), using a striking, highly Gombrowiczian metaphor, by suggesting that *Ferdydurke* was "an inventory of the pantry, the back staircase of the self."

This philosophical background of the novel (which is not without analogy with the world of seventeenth-century moralists such as Pascal and La Rochefoucauld) has its aesthetic counterpart: the novel should also free itself from convention to invent its own form. For the subversive, debunking aspect of his system, Gombrowicz would argue along with Augustine that the artist should begin his creation by creating himself.

The prose of *Ferdydurke* matches in creativity the humor and truculence of its subject matter. As has been pointed out by Danuta Borchardt, its first English translator from the original Polish, it resorts to four different linguistic registers: literary, colloquial, upper-class, and peasant. In addition, for *Ferdydurke,* Gombrowicz invents its own language by distorting idioms and common usage. This linguistic complexity has made it a particularly challenging work to render into other tongues.

Passport photograph of Gombrowicz in 1939.

After the publication of *Ferdydurke,* Gombrowicz travelled to Italy. He later told Dominique de Roux that he did not bother to visit St. Peter's because, as he explained to a Lithuanian painter he encountered in Rome, "all churches are the same inside." But he noticed with alarm the rise of fascism, especially on his return journey through Austria, which coincided with Hitler's entry into Vienna following the *Anschluss.* He then took a long rest in the Tatra Mountains before returning to Warsaw.

Opetani, Gombrowicz's second novel, occupies an odd place in his oeuvre. It was as if, having contributed to the most avant-gardist modernity with *Ferdydurke,* he had decided to pay tribute to what would be described, from a modernist viewpoint, as bad—or non-literary—literature. According to Herling-Grudzinski's *Dziennik pisany noca* (Diary written at night), the novel was undertaken as a result of a bet that he was capable of producing a good example of the kind of book enjoyed by a mass readership. Accordingly, *Opetani* (rendered in English as *Possessed*) was serialized simultaneously in two newspapers, the evening daily *Dobry Wieczor! Kurier Czernowy* in Warsaw and the morning daily *Express Poranny* in Kielce-Radom. The publication began on 4 June 1939 and the last installment came out on 3 September,

FROM *Ferdydurke*

Oh, the power of Form! Nations die because of it. It is the cause of wars. It creates something in us that is not of us. If you make light of it you'll never understand stupidity nor evil nor crime. It governs our slightest impulses. It is at the base of our collective life. For you, however, Form and Style still belong strictly to the realm of the aesthetic—for you style is on paper only, in the style of your stories. Gentlemen, who will slap your pupa which you dare turn toward others as you kneel at the altar of art? For you form is not something that is human and alive, something—I'd say—practical and everyday, but just a feature for the holidays. And while you're leaning over a piece of paper you forget your own self—you don't care about perfecting your own individual and concrete style, you merely practice an abstract stylization in a vacuum. Instead of art serving you, you serve art—and with a sheeplike docility you let it impede your development, and you let it push you into the hell of indolence.

Now consider how different the stance would be of someone who, instead of feeding on the words of the concept makers, would sweep the world with a fresh look and with an understanding of the boundless importance of form in our lives. If he were to take up the pen it would not be for the sake of becoming an Artist but—let's say—to better express his individuality and explain it to others; or else to put his internal affairs in order, and also, perhaps, to deepen and sharpen his relationship with his fellow men because other souls exert an immense and creative influence on our soul; or, for example, to try to fight for a world as he would like it to be, for a world that is indispensable to his life. He would, of course, spare no effort to have his work attract people and win their hearts with its artistic charm—but in this case his chief goal would be not art but the expression of his own person. And I say "his own," not "someone else's," because it's high time you stopped this thinking of yourselves as creatures of a higher order who are here to edify and enlighten someone else, to lead and raise someone else into the sublime, or to improve someone else's morals. Who has granted you this superiority? Where does it say that you now belong to a higher class? Who has promoted you to aristocracy? Who gave you a patent on Maturity?

Preface to "The Child Runs Deep in Filidor," from *Ferdydurke*, translated by Danuta Borchardt, New Haven and London: Yale University Press, 2000.

the day Britain and France declared war on Germany following the invasion of Poland by Hitler's army two days before.

Gombrowicz published *Opetani* under the pseudonym Z. Niewieski. Suggested by his brother Jerzy, it was coined after the Lithuanian river Niewiaza. Nor did Gombrowicz mention *Opetani* afterwards (there is nothing about it in his published conversations with Dominique de Roux) until the one reference in the otherwise none too reliable chronology he prepared at the end of his life for de Roux's Cahier de l'Herne (though, in this instance, he gets both the year and the title of the daily wrong). Was Gombrowicz uneasy, for aesthetic reasons, about a work he remembered as a semi-failure, as Jelenski has argued? Or was he embarrassed, as his brother Jerzy has suggested, because of the generous royalties he received for delighting cab drivers and greengrocers, by contrast with the misunderstood, largely self-sponsored *Ferdydurke*?

When *Opetani* was first published in book form by the Paris-based émigré publishing house Kultura in 1973 as part of the volume *Varia,* it lacked the last three episodes. These, which had appeared only in the *Kurier Warszawski* for 1, 2, and 3 September 1939, were discovered by Ludwik Grzeniewski in 1986 and published in October of that year in the Warsaw weekly *Argumenty*. The first complete Polish edition of *Opetani* came out in Warsaw in 1994. The English version published by Calder and Boyars was based on the incomplete French text of 1977 that was serialized in *Le Monde* before its appearance in book form.

Opetani, Gombrowicz's longest novel, is part detective fiction, part horror story, part psychological thriller. It exhibits many trappings of the genre popularized in the early twentieth century by Conan Doyle in England and by the Fantômas, Rouletabille, and Belphégor series in France: a haunted castle full of unsuspected treasures; a mad prince manipulated by an unscrupulous secretary; an eccentric Polish-American millionaire found murdered, in the best *Mystère de la chambre jaune* tradition, in a room locked from the inside. The plot is full of loose ends and red herrings, not all of which are eventually explained. The narration, told from the point of view of an omniscient narrator, has an endearing over-the-top, improvisatory quality. Yet, as Jelenski has demonstrated, many quintessential Gombrowiczian features are present: the heroine and hero, Maya and Marian (Gombrowicz's middle name), whose youth and purity stand out against the artificiality and corruption of the world surrounding them; the satire of Warsaw's upper classes; the highly evocative accounts of tennis matches, a favorite sport of Gombrowicz's during his Polish years. The Gombrowicz of *Iwona* and *Ferdydurke*—and of the future *Diary*—is also recognizable in the recurrent themes of suffering and cruelty, as in the book's most memorable episode, when Marian, after showing his kind-heartedness by rescuing a squirrel threatened by the evil Kholawitski, is provoked into smashing the innocent creature against a tree.

From the exhibition:

Photograph of the Gombrowicz house in Maloszyce.

Manuscript autobiographical notes, n.d. [1950s or early 1960s?]

Family tree, typescript with autograph corrections, n.d. [1950s?]

Photograph of Gombrowicz at Maloszyce in 1910.

Photograph of Gombrowicz and his siblings at Potoczek in 1928.

Portrait of Bruno Schulz by S. L. Witkiewicz (1935) and photograph of Schulz in 1934, from Jerzy Ficowski, ed., *Bruno Schulz Ksiega listów* (Cracow: Wydawnictwo Literackie, n.d.).

Ferdydurke. Warsaw: Towarzystwo Wydawnicze "Rój," 1938 [actually issued in 1937]. From the library of Witold Gombrowicz.

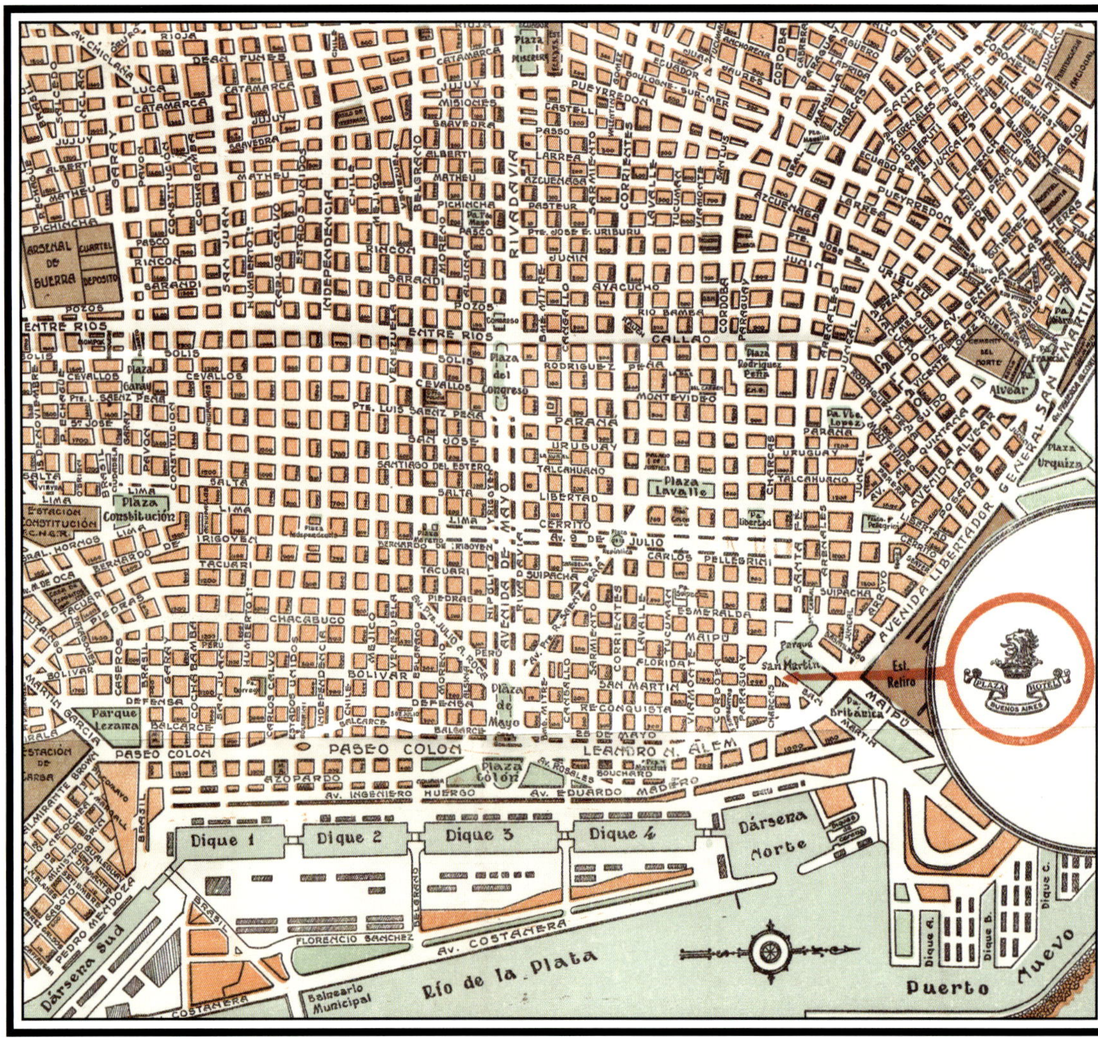

Buenos Aires, ca. 1955.

CHAPTER TWO Witoldo, 1939–63

On 1 August 1939, Gombrowicz sailed for Argentina on the maiden voyage of the liner *Boleslaw Chrobry*, which inaugurated a new Atlantic crossing between the Polish port Gdynia and Buenos Aires. In later life, he always maintained that this departure, which was to transform the course of his life, was due to chance: a fellow writer, the novelist Czeslaw Straszewicz (1915–62), who was among the various personalities invited by the company to participate in the voyage, got him invited as well. The *Chrobry* arrived in Buenos Aires on 21 August to an official welcome from the Polish diplomatic mission and the émigré Polish community. Two days later, the Soviet Union signed the pact of non-aggression with Germany. The threat of war being imminent, the *Chrobry* was ordered to sail back to Poland. At the last minute, Gombrowicz decided to disembark and stay in Argentina until the end of the hostilities, which began on 1 September. As it happened, he was to remain in Latin America for more than twenty-three years and was never to set foot in Poland again.

Just when his literary career in Poland was beginning to take hold, Gombrowicz found himself in a foreign land, of which he did not even speak the language, without resources or prospects, and cut off from his native country by the war, followed by the Communist takeover and the Cold War. The first six or seven years of his exile were, from both an economic and a moral point of view, the most difficult of his life. They are also the most mysterious, during which he produced no work of substance. Yet, paradoxically, he came to see his new situation as a liberation from any ties—cultural as well as material—to the old order. Having first lived in a series of modest pensiones in the center of Buenos Aires, Gombrowicz exhausted in six months the 200 dollars he had with him when he landed. His gold watch was stolen from him. Through Jeremi Stempowski, the head of the Gdynia America Line, he was introduced to established Argentinian writers such as Arturo Capdevila (1889–1966) and Manuel Gálvez (1882–1962), who in turn recommended him to newspapers and arranged for him to give lectures (in French) on literary topics. At the end of 1940, also through Stempowski's intercession, he received financial help from the Furstemberg family, which in early 1942 arranged for him to obtain a modest pension from the Polish embassy for a few months. In early

1943, unable to pay his rent, he clandestinely left his lodgings at 242 Tacuari and moved in with an equally impoverished, indebted compatriot in Moron, in the suburbs, where, as he later told Dominique de Roux, he slept on the floor for six months, while the villa was visited at night by angry creditors helping themselves to his roommate's possessions. He also recalled having to satisfy his hunger by attending funerals in order to partake of the ensuing buffets. Gombrowicz's freedom from the old world took another form with the homosexual adventures he enjoyed throughout that period, mostly with young workers, soldiers, and sailors in the part of town known as the Retiro, where the main train station and the harbor are situated. Understandably reticent on the subject in his published *Diary*, Gombrowicz eventually acknowledged his bisexuality in the chronology he wrote in 1969 for the Cahier de l'Herne. Several of his works have a clear homoerotic subtext. In his testimony for Rita Gombrowicz, the Argentinian writer Ernesto Sábato has claimed that Gombrowicz had planned to write an account of his homosexual years, suggesting that he had in it a masterpiece to rival Jean Genet's work.

The Gran Rex café on Corrientes, Buenos Aires.
Photo: Rita Gombrowicz

By 1941, Gombrowicz had enough Spanish to contribute pseudonymous articles and tales to various Argentinian periodicals, for which he was helped by the Argentinian novelist and critic Roger Plá (1912–82). He became an habitué of several cafés, notably the Gran Rex, on Avenida Corrientes, where the Polish-born Paolino Frydman founded and headed a chess academy, in which Gombrowicz was a regular participant until its closure in 1961.

The El Querandi café, on Perú at Moreno, another Buenos Aires café patronized by Gombrowicz.
Photo: Rita Gombrowicz

Gombrowicz's material situation improved in 1943 when he started collaborating with the Jesuit periodical *Solidaridad* and the Catholic journal *Criterio*, where, in January 1944, he published an article on "Catholicism before the new tendencies in art" under the pen name Mariano Lenogiry (the name of one of his grandfather's Lithuanian estates). Three months later, the literary magazine *Papeles de Buenos Aires*, edited by the lawyer and essayist Adolfo de Obieta, published "Filidor forrado de nino," the Spanish version of the story incorporated in *Ferdydurke*.

Prepared by Gombrowicz himself with the help of a few friends, the translation paved the way for the more ambitious project of tackling the whole book. In November 1945, Gombrowicz obtained from his friend Cecilia Benedit de Benedetti an allowance in order to devote himself to the Spanish translation

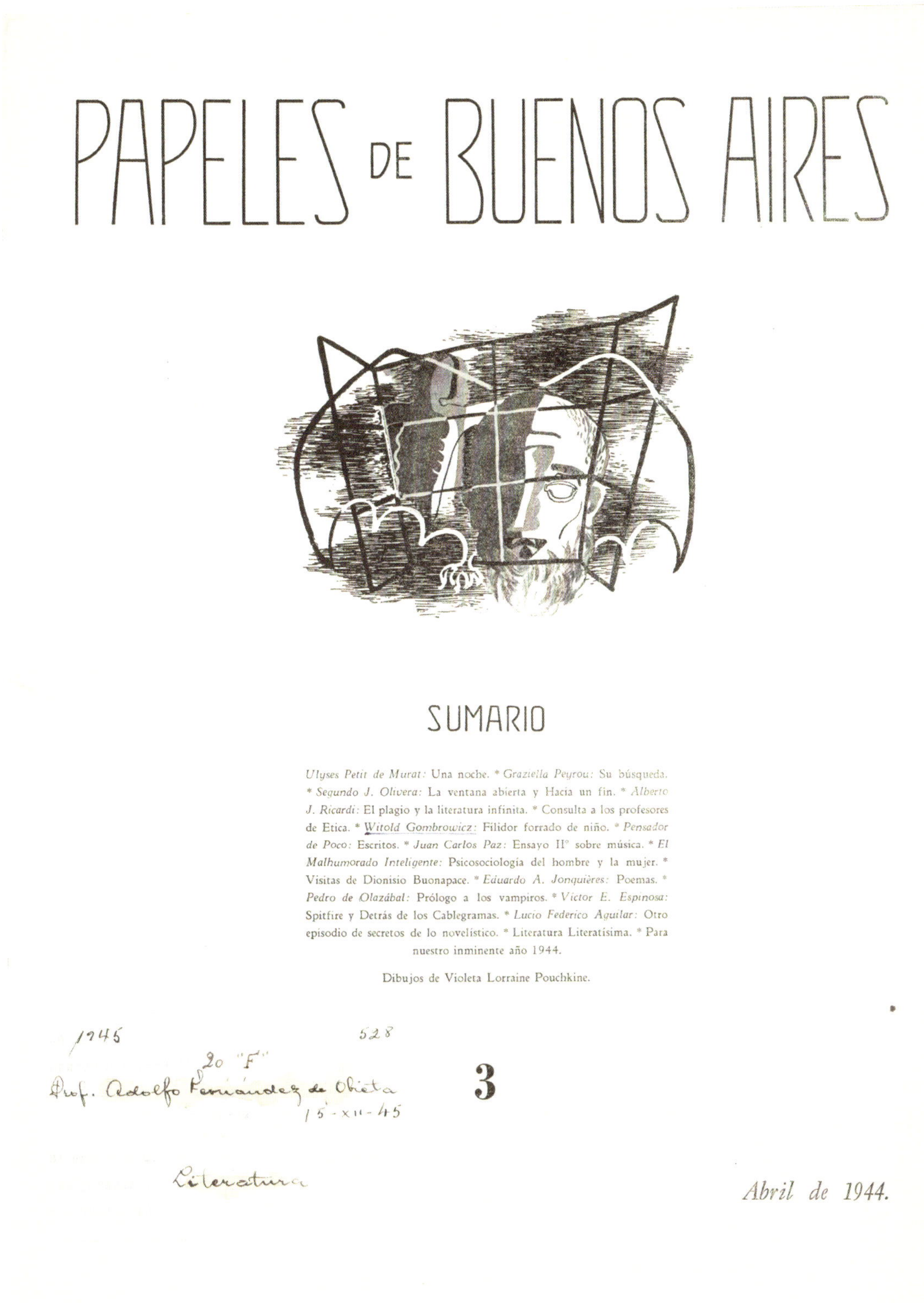

PAPELES DE BUENOS AIRES

SUMARIO

Ulyses Petit de Murat: Una noche. * *Graziella Peyrou:* Su búsqueda. * *Segundo J. Olivera:* La ventana abierta y Hacia un fin. * *Alberto J. Ricardi:* El plagio y la literatura infinita. * Consulta a los profesores de Etica. * *Witold Gombrowicz:* Filidor forrado de niño. * *Pensador de Poco:* Escritos. * *Juan Carlos Paz:* Ensayo II° sobre música. * *El Malhumorado Inteligente:* Psicosociología del hombre y la mujer. * Visitas de Dionisio Buonapace. * *Eduardo A. Jonquières:* Poemas. * *Pedro de Olazábal:* Prólogo a los vampiros. * *Victor E. Espinosa:* Spitfire y Detrás de los Cablegramas. * *Lucio Federico Aguilar:* Otro episodio de secretos de lo novelístico. * Literatura Literatísima. * Para nuestro inminente año 1944.

Dibujos de Violeta Lorraine Pouchkine.

3

Abril de 1944.

Papeles de Buenos Aires, no. 3 (April 1944), contained "Filidor forrado de nino."

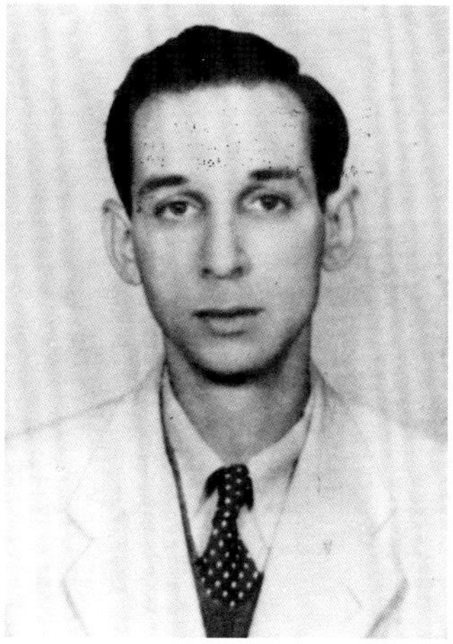

Virgilio Piñera in 1946.

of *Ferdydurke*. It occupied him and thirteen others for the next eighteen months. One of the participants in the project, Adolfo de Obieta, later declared: "The translation of *Ferdydurke* is one of the most amusing and curious I know, transposing from Polish into Spanish the book of a Polish author who barely knew Spanish, assisted by five or six Latino-Americans who scarcely knew two words of Polish." The work was begun in predictably disorganized fashion during sessions that took place in the chess room on the second floor of the Rex. Among the members of the group was Gombrowicz's cousin Gustaw Kotkowski, who had resided in Buenos Aires since July 1940. Its chief mover, however, was the Cuban writer Virgilio Piñera (1912–79), who arrived in Buenos Aires in February 1946 with the fellow writer and his lover Humberto Rodriguez Tomeu (born in 1919) and took over the project. Piñera and Rodriguez Tomeu remained in the Argentinian capital until December 1947 and devoted themselves, through most of 1946, to revising and completing the translation, a daunting task given the unconventional language of the original, not to mention the absence of a Polish-Spanish dictionary. Piñera's short stories and plays later made him one of the leading Cuban writers of the post-war period until he fell foul with Fidel Castro in the late 1960s. His role in the Spanish translation of *Ferdydurke* can be compared to the one Valery Larbaud had played in the French *Ulysses*.

The Spanish *Ferdydurke*, issued in April 1947, had a preface by Gombrowicz—in which Piñera is singled out as president of the translation committee—and a dedication to Cecilia de Benedetti, by the Buenos Aires publishing house Argos, with which a contract had been signed in November of the previous year. Despite the efforts of Gombrowicz and his friends, as documented in the manuscript "Ferdydurke Chronicle" preserved in the archive, the book was largely ignored by the Argentinian literary circles, while many of those who took notice objected to the translation on linguistic grounds. Yet Gombrowicz received an enthusiastic letter from Gálvez, in which the Argentinian novelist compared the work to Rabelais and the Marinetti of *Le roi Bombance*, while finding Gombrowicz's psychological insights worthy of Proust or Stendhal.

Its lack of success notwithstanding, the translation of *Ferdydurke* marked the resumption of Gombrowicz's literary activity on a large scale. He continued it with *Slub* (*The marriage*). By his own account, he started drafting the play in 1944, but it was written

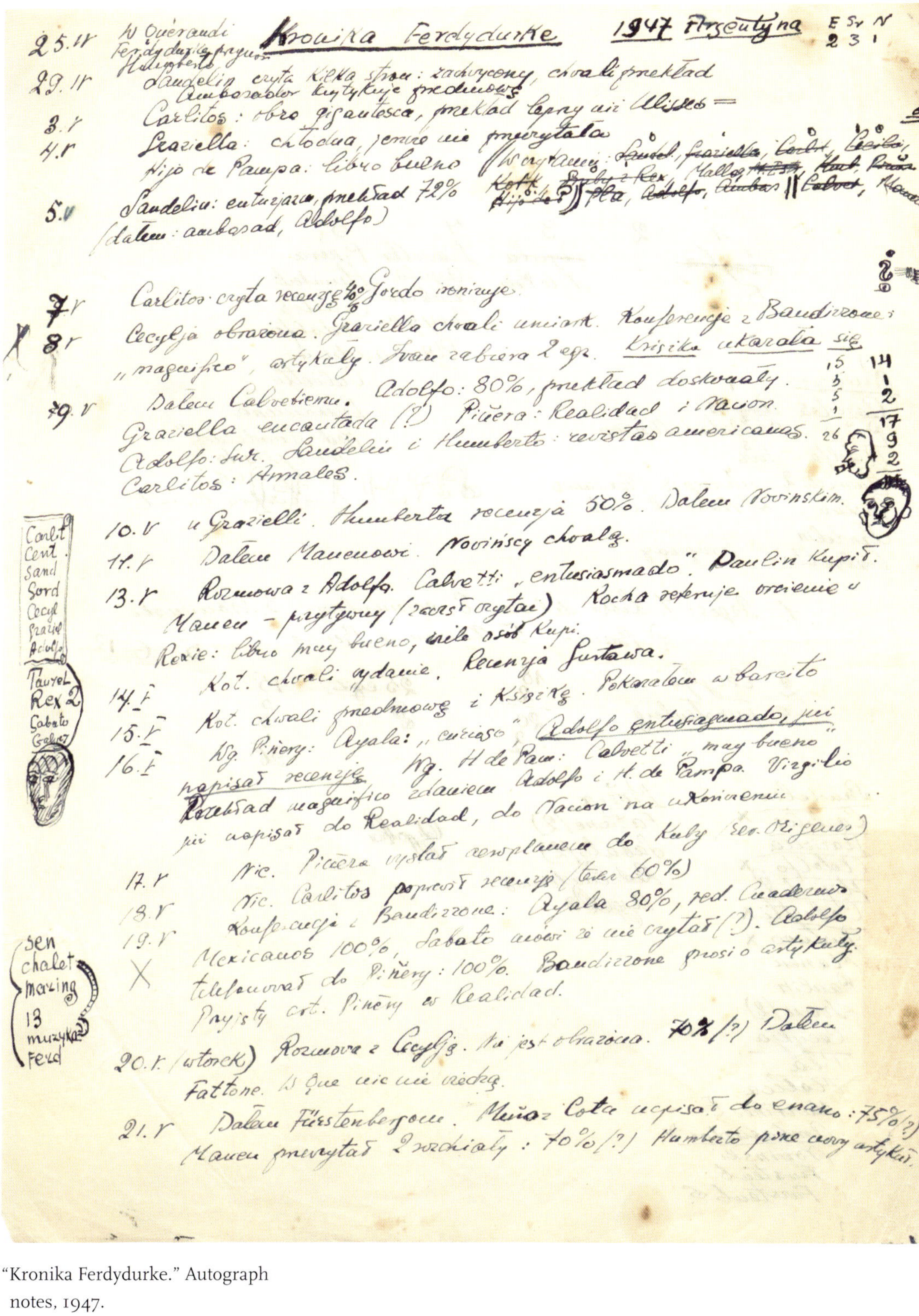

"Kronika Ferdydurke." Autograph notes, 1947.

chiefly in late 1946 and in the first months of 1947 when recuperating in the mountains of Córdoba, where his friend Cecilia de Benedetti owned ranches. In Polish, "Slub" refers to the exchange of vows rather than to the institution of marriage. Gombrowicz, however, preferred it to be called in English *The marriage* rather than *The wedding* in order to avoid confusion with the 1901 play by Stanislaw Wyspianski. Gombrowicz's work could be subtitled "The soldier's dream." Henry, the hero, is a young Pole fighting on the French front at the beginning of World War II. Reunited with his longtime friend Johnny, he finds himself in an abandoned house, where he has a vision of his native home at Maloszyce (Gombrowicz's own birthplace). Indeed, Henry's parents soon appear, as does his sweetheart Molly. But the father has become an innkeeper, rudely treated by his drunken patrons, and Molly a servant and a slut. When Henry kneels in front of his father to protect him from the drunks, they start calling the latter a king, a joke that, despite Henry's resistance, takes on an absurd reality of its own. The newly crowned king promises his son a solemn wedding, to be consecrated by a bishop. But the wedding preparations are interrupted by the return of the chief drunkard, now the ambassador of a hostile power (the character has been interpreted as standing for Hitler). Under his advice, Henry has his father arrested and proclaims himself king. Having freed himself from paternal and divine authority, he plans to confer the sacrament of marriage upon himself. As the wedding approaches, however, he begins to suspect that Molly and Johnny are having an affair and confronts them. He then persuades Johnny to kill himself. Johnny's corpse is discovered as the ceremony is about to proceed. The marriage never takes place.

Gombrowicz's most complex play, *The marriage*, with its oneiric, discontinued elements, strongly invites comparison with the so-called Theater of the Absurd, as illustrated by Beckett, Ionesco, and Adamov, none of whom were active as playwrights when *Slub* was written. While later rejecting any association with those authors, Gombrowicz nonetheless characterized his play as "obscure, somnambulistic, extravagant," suggesting that he himself could not "decipher it entirely." He also admitted that he had set out to write a "great play" in the tradition of Shakespeare and Goethe. The violence of the plot and the language do indeed bring to mind *Hamlet* and *King Lear*, while the play has an allegorical quality that may evoke *Faust*. Written without any prospect of it being performed in the foreseeable future, *The marriage*—

as the transparent autobiographical allusions imply—also owes something to Gombrowicz's physical and spiritual exile. According to Milosz, he considered it his favorite among his works. In the *Entretiens* with Dominique de Roux, he admitted that he wrote it in a state of despair, to which the tragedy of the war evidently contributed. The war affected his family directly since his brother Janusz and nephew Józef, captured by the Germans after the Warsaw uprising, were deported to Auschwitz and Mauthausen, though they miraculously survived.

Throughout his Argentinian years, Gombrowicz kept his distance from the local literary establishment, dominated by Victoria Ocampo and the journal *Sur*, which she had founded in 1931. Gombrowicz came closest to this circle through his friendship with the poet Carlos Mastronardi (1901–76). In his *Diary*, Gombrowicz recalls a dinner hosted by Silvina Ocampo, Victoria's younger sister, and her husband the writer Adolfo Bioy Casares, at which Jorge Luis Borges was present—as were José Bianco and Mastronardi. While Bianco, who many years later translated *Opetani* into Spanish, was drawn to Gombrowicz, Borges showed little interest in the work of the Polish writer. As for Gombrowicz, while admiring Borges, he often reproached the Argentinian intelligentsia publicly (for example in the article "Cuatro respuestas de Witold Gombrowicz" he published in April 1949 in the journal *9 Artes*) for its inhibiting fascination with Europe, and especially Paris, contrasting it with his own interest in Argentina and its youth. On 28 August 1947, Gombrowicz delivered his famous polemical lecture "Contra los poetas" at Fray Mocho, a bookstore-cum-literary café popular with the literary bohème of Buenos Aires. The original Spanish version of this talk, preserved in the Beinecke Library, remains unpublished. Gombrowicz expounded on a theme already present in the school scenes of *Ferdydurke*: poetry, he argues, is something we claim to admire because we are told to, or out of a respect for tradition that owes nothing to aesthetic or intellectual values, like the passive belief in an established cult. This apparent dismissal of poetry is, in fact, a plea for freedom from unquestioned literary conventions and for independence of judgment, parallel to Gombrowicz's denunciation of the Argentinian intelligentsia's dependency on European models. The talk was illustrated by examples in Spanish, read by Piñera, who had selected them with Rodriguez Tomeu. Gombrowicz, who had originally intended to submit "Contra los poetas" to *Sur*, revised it for the Polish version he published in *Kultura* in 1951 and republished, in book form, at the end of the first volume of his *Diary*.

The house at 615 Venezuela,
Buenos Aires.
Photo: Rita Gombrowicz

The youngest member of the *Ferdydurke* translation committee was an Argentinian student of philosophy, of Serbian and Italian background, named Alejandro Rússovich. He had entered Gombrowicz's life in the spring of 1946 and eventually (after the period of their closest intimacy) became his roommate at 615 Venezuela, which was Gombrowicz's address from February 1945 until his departure from Argentina 18 years later. Rússovich's invaluable testimony, published in *Gombrowicz en Argentine,* offers the most complete portrait we have of the writer in the early 1950s.

Between April and August 1948, under Gombrowicz's guidance, Rússovich translated *The marriage* into Spanish. Entitled *El casamiento* and with a preface written directly in Spanish by Gombrowicz, the play came out under the imprint of the musical publishing house EAM, which Cecilia de Benedetti had founded in 1945. It was the only purely literary book issued by the firm. As Rússovich bitterly recalled in the testimony he later wrote for Rita Gombrowicz, the publication of *El casamiento* met with complete indifference, eliciting not a single review. Gombrowicz had also sent the Polish text of the play to his sister Irena, but despite the efforts and encouragements of friends and fellow writers in Poland, notably the novelist Maria Kuncewicz, there were no prospects for the play to be published there. Gombrowicz had given it to Iwaszkiewicz as well when he visited Argentina in 1948—"an unforgettable visit," as Gombrowicz later recalled. However, as Iwaszkiewicz laconically reported to Gombrowicz in January 1949, the lack of an ostensible element of social satire made *The marriage* unpalatable in the context of Zhdanovian social realism to which Eastern Europe was subjected in the decade following the end of the war. The only text Gombrowicz published in Poland in that period was a moving "Letter to Ferdydurkists," which appeared in 1947 in the periodical *Nowiny Literackie,* then edited by Iwaszkiewicz, whose daughters were the addressees of this open letter.

The extent to which Gombrowicz suffered in isolation from his native country was revealed in 1970 by the unauthorized publication of his letters to Iwaszkiewicz, which showed that he tried to obtain a position as cultural attaché in Buenos Aires and suggested that *Ferdydurke* be republished in Poland with a preface emphasizing its satirical element. After losing hope of having *The marriage* published in Poland, Gombrowicz circulated typescript copies of the play. One was sent to Martin Buber

El casamiento. Buenos Aires: Ediciones EAM, 1948. From the library of Witold Gombrowicz.

(1878–1965), the Polish-born philosopher, then living in Israel, who responded in July 1951 with a letter of praise. Gombrowicz also prepared, in May 1949, a French translation with two young French women, daughters of diplomats posted in Buenos Aires. Revised with the assistance of a *Paris-Match* journalist, this translation (which remains unpublished) was sent, without eliciting any reactions, to André Gide, Albert Camus, and Jean-Louis Barrault, with whom Gombrowicz had a cordial meeting when the French actor-director and his touring company performed the adaptation of Kafka's *The trial* in Buenos Aires. Gombrowicz had better luck with his compatriots living in the United States, where the play attracted the attention of Czeslaw Milosz, then cultural attaché to the Polish embassy in Washington (he defected in February 1951). Milosz in turn brought *The marriage* to the attention of the poet and novelist Józef Wittlin (1896–1976), who had settled in New York after the war, and in whom Gombrowicz was to find a loyal ally. In January 1951, Wittlin wrote Gombrowicz an enthusiastic letter about *The marriage*, urging his correspondent to contact Jerzy Giedroyc and Czapski to have it published by *Kultura*.

Gombrowicz with colleagues at the Banco polaco, Buenos Aires.

Gombrowicz's financial circumstances took a new turn in December 1947 when he was hired as personal assistant to the director of the Banco polaco, the Argentinian branch of the Polish Savings Bank, nationalized in 1945. The Banco polaco had about thirty employees, all Poles, and occupied an elegant mansion at 462 Tucuman, in the business district of Buenos Aires. Thanks to the protection and understanding of Juliusz Nowinski, the director, Gombrowicz was actually able to devote part of his time at the bank to his own writing, and it was chiefly there that he wrote his third novel, *Trans-Atlantyk*.

Like *Ferdydurke, Trans-Atlantyk* is narrated in the first person. The autobiographical element, in fact, dominates the beginning of the book, which purports to be the adventures of a Polish writer named Witold Gombrowicz in and around Buenos Aires in the fall of 1939, beginning with his decision not to return to Poland. The version given in the novel, however, is distorted for polemical purposes. The Gombrowicz of *Trans-Atlantyk* anathemizes his country ("Holy Slug" is one of many apostrophes) and poses as a deserter. The real Gombrowicz was nothing of the sort: matriculated at the Polish Consulate, he volunteered to enlist in December 1942 when Poles living abroad were mobilized, to be turned down for health reasons. In keeping with this deliberately misleading self-presentation, the Polish officials in Buenos Aires are portrayed in *Trans-Atlantyk* in a gleefully satirical, caricatural fashion. In his efforts to escape from what he views as empty nationalistic posturing on the part of his compatriots, the narrator comes into contact with the impersonation of its polar opposite: Gonzalo, a wealthy middle-aged Argentine homosexual (identified throughout by the derogatory term "Puto"), whose life is devoted to the cult of pleasure and beauty, whether cruising the streets of Buenos Aires or recuperating in his luxurious *estancia* outside the city. But the two worlds—the old world of traditional values and the hedonistic world of Gonzalo—are brought into conflict when the object of Puto's desire turns out to be a young Polish soldier named Ignacy, whose father Tomasz is the incarnation of honor, patriotism, and moral rectitude. "Gombrowicz," while reluctant to betray the traditional values of the fatherland, finds himself irresistibly attracted by those of the

Trans-Atlantyk — Slub. Z komentarzem autora. Warsaw: Czytelnik, 1957. From the library of Witold Gombrowicz.

"sonland" advocated by Gonzalo (Carolyn French's and Nina Karsov's English translation felicitously renders the opposition as "Patria" versus "Filistria"). After a burlesque duel between Gonzalo and Tomasz, witnessed by the Polish officials masquerading as a hunting party, the novel ends, in the manner of *Ferdydurke*, in a carnivalesque ball at Gonzalo's *estancia*, where, in a dazzling display of linguistic virtuosity, the dilemma is left unresolved. *Trans-Atlantyk*, which became available in English only in 1994, is the most difficult of Gombrowicz's novels to translate. Its style, reminiscent in its use of invective of the post-war novels of Louis-Ferdinand Céline, is actually derived from an old Polish tradition: the seventeenth-century baroque narratives, halfway between oral tradition and writing, resurrected by Adam Mickiewicz in his 1834 epic poem *Pan Tadeusz*. *Trans-Atlantyk* is, in Gombrowicz's own words, "a Pan Tadeusz in reverse": whereas Mickiewicz aims at a patriotic reconciliation of opposites, Gombrowicz is not afraid to expose and ridicule some of the values and attitudes held dear by many members of the Polish émigré community.

This corrosive, provocative book—which the poet, critic, and translator Stanislaw Baranczak has called Gombrowicz's "greatest accomplishment as an artist"—marked his sensational reentry into Polish letters. It was serialized in May and June 1951 in

Kultura, to the indignation of many of its readers, for most of whom Gombrowicz was just a provocateur out of nowhere (significantly, the first episode was preceded by an editorial note explaining who Gombrowicz was). *Kultura*, launched in June 1947 in Rome, was the organ of the Instytut Literacki, founded by a group of Polish intellectuals who had fought against the Axis in the army of General Anders: Jerzy Giedroyc (1906–2000), Zygmunt Hertz (1908–79) and his wife Zofia (1911–2003), the painter Józef Czapski (1896–1993), and the essayist Gustaw Herling-Grudzinski (1919–2000). In the summer of 1947, the Literary Institute established its headquarters in Maisons-Laffitte, the Paris suburb, where it acquired a house in 1954. By then, *Kultura* had become not just the leading literary journal of the Polish emigration, but one of the outstanding intellectual periodicals of the post-war period. After the scandal caused by the serialization of *Trans-Atlantyk* in *Kultura*, Wittlin came to Gombrowicz's defense in an "Apology of Gombrowicz," published in the July–August 1951 issue of the journal. A reworked version of this essay subsequently served as the preface to the first book edition of *Trans-Atlantyk* and *The marriage*, which came out in 1953. This volume, the first to be issued under the Kultura imprint (the second was Milosz's *The captive mind*), was also Gombrowicz's first book in Polish since the publication of *Ferdydurke* in 1937. In the preface, which Gombrowicz described in his *Diary* as "a miracle of clear persuasion and kindness, dynamic in the most modern sense," Wittlin explained that Gombrowicz's writings "have such an explosive force that they upset all our intellectual and affective resources." The book introduced Gombrowicz to a new generation of Polish readers.

The year 1953, the fourteenth of Gombrowicz's exile, was the great turning point in his career. Beginning in April 1953, he started, at Giedroyc's prompting, a monthly contribution to *Kultura* in the form of a diary, which continued until his death in 1969. Originally inspired by Gide's journal, Gombrowicz's diary is not a diary in the intimate sense. There are, indeed, autobiographical passages, both current and retrospective, but, by Gombrowicz's own admission, they should not always be taken literally. (He later acknowledged in "Argentine peregrinations" that his account of his boat trip up the Rio Paraná was partly fictional.) The few long-hand manuscript fragments that survive in the archive show how artfully he used the supposedly spontaneous form of the diary: even the dates, usually not a date but the day of the week, turn out to be arbitrary, as if they were there just to

FROM *Diary*

TUESDAY.

Something happened yesterday... something like a continuation of the dog at the *estancia*.... And if I said that there is nothing equal somehow to the repugnance of the dilemma that I experienced ... that I found myself where humanity must retch.... I could say this. I could also torment myself with it—it is really up to me.

I was lying in the sun, cleverly concealed in the mountain chain the sand forms when blown by the wind to the edges of the beach. These are mountains of sand, dunes, abundant in ravines, slopes, valleys, a curving and shifting labyrinth, overgrown here and there with brush that vibrates under the unceasing toil of the wind. I was shielded by a substantial *Jungfrau*, nobly cubic, proud—when one of those hurricanes that endlessly lash this scorched Sahara kicked up about ten centimeters from my nose. Some sort of beetles—I don't know what to call them—bustled along this desert for reasons unknown. And one of them, within my reach, lay upside down. The wind had overturned it. The sun beat on its belly, which certainly must have been unpleasant considering that this belly was usually left in the shade—there he lay, thrashing his little legs—and it was obvious that nothing was left to it except a monotonous and desperate thrashing of its legs—and it was growing weak, perhaps it had been there for hours; it was dying.

I, a giant, inaccessible to him in my enormity, an enormity that made me invisible to it—I watched that thrashing of legs ... and extending my hand, extricated him from his agony. He moved ahead, returned to life in a split second.

I had barely done this when I noticed a little farther away, an identical beetle in an identical predicament. And he, too, was thrashing his little legs. I didn't want to move.... But—why did you save that little guy and not this one?... Why that one ... when this one?... You make one happy and the other should suffer? I took a stick, extended my hand—and saved him.

I had barely done this when I saw, somewhat farther, an identical beetle in an identical predicament. Thrashing his little legs. And the sun was beating down on his belly.

Was I supposed to change my siesta into an ambulance for beetles in their death throes? But I had become too friendly with these beetles, in their strangely helpless thrashing... and you will probably understand that once I had started this rescuing, I had no right to stop at some arbitrary point. It would have been an awful thing to do to this third beetle—to stop exactly at the threshold of his defeat ... too cruel and somehow impossible to do.... Bah! if there had been some sort of boundary between him and the ones I rescued, something that could have authorized me to stop—but there was absolutely nothing, only another ten centimeters of sand, always the same bit of sand, "a little farther away," it is true, but only "a little." And he waved his little legs in the same way! Looking around, however, I noticed "just a little" farther, another four beetles, thrashing and being scorched by the sun—there was no helping it. I got up and rescued them all. Off they went.

Then what should my eyes behold but the gleaming-hot-sandy plane of a neighboring slope and on it five or six little thrashing dots: beetles. I rushed to their rescue. I saved them. And by this time I was so wrapped up in their suffering, I was so absorbed by it, that, seeing new beetles all along the plains, ravines, and canyons, an endless rash of tortured dots, I began to walk the sands as if I were demented, rescuing, rescuing, rescuing!

From *Diary (1957–1961)*, translated by Lillian Vallee, Evanston: Northwestern University Press, 1989.

remind the reader that the text is a diary. This largely artificial spontaneity allows Gombrowicz greater freedom in polemical discussions and philosophical and moral digressions in the manner of Montaigne. Yet the tone, with its mixture of intellectual brilliance and sardonic humor, belongs to Gombrowicz alone, making his diary one of the great examples of the genre.

It was also in 1953 that Jelenski began a campaign to get Gombrowicz's works published and recognized in Western Europe. Born in 1922, Jelenski, officially the son of a Polish diplomat, was actually the natural son of Count Carlo Sforza, Italian minister of foreign affairs under Mussolini, with whom he broke, to be restored to his ministerial post after the war. Educated at Oxford, Jelenski joined the Polish Legion in 1944. In 1952, after several years in Italy, where he worked for various international agencies, Jelenski settled in the French capital with the Argentinian-born painter of Italian origin, Leonor Fini (1908–96). An essayist, art critic, and translator, Jelenski was involved in the Congress for Cultural Freedom, the international non-governmental agency created in 1949—under covert sponsorship of the CIA, as it transpired much later—to mobilize intellectuals against Communist totalitarianism. Jelenski was closely associated with *Preuves*, the French literary journal published by the Congress (its English equivalent was *Encounter*). Having read *Ferdydurke* in Spanish at Jelenski's prompting, François Bondy, the German-Hungarian, French-educated editor of *Preuves*, published a note on the novel in its October 1953 issue. This first commentary to appear in Western Europe was followed two months later by Jelenski's more developed analysis in the same journal.

Jelenski, who died in 1987, is now justly regarded as one of the key figures of the Polish emigration. He became a close intellectual ally of its greatest painter (Czapski), its greatest novelist and playwright (Gombrowicz), and its greatest poet (Milosz). Czapski and Gombrowicz, whom the painter saw in 1955 in Buenos Aires, where he had relatives, never had an easy relationship. As for Milosz and Gombrowicz, they were not close and did not even meet until very late in Gombrowicz's life; but they had considerable esteem for each other despite philosophical differences. A few years after Gombrowicz's death, Milosz reflected on those differences in his 1975 essay entitled (after Blake) *The land of Ulro*.

After the completion of *Trans-Atlantyk*, Gombrowicz, still at the Banco polaco, began a play that he entitled *Historia* (*History*)

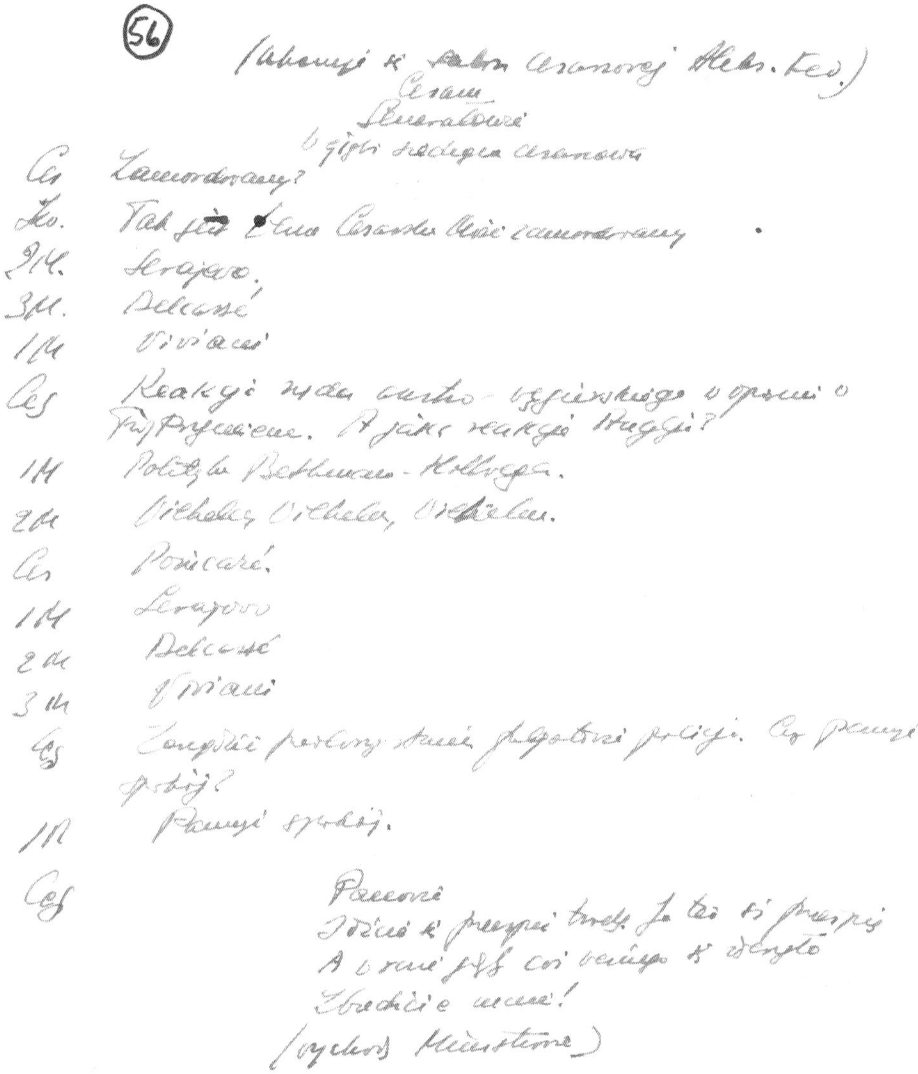

Historia. Manuscript fragment of this unfinished play [1951].

and subtitled “an operetta.” Suspicious of opera, too grandiloquent for his taste, Gombrowicz was fond of operetta, a genre he later described to Bondy as “a marvellous theatrical form, of divine stupidity, magically grotesque and petrified.” (In the opening sentence of his earliest published story, “Lawyer Kraykowski’s dancer,” the first-person narrator informs us that he is attending his thirty-fourth performance of Emmerich Kálmán’s *Die Csárdásfürstin*.) Gombrowicz wrote several incomplete drafts of *Historia* before abandoning the project. After his death, they were discovered in his papers by Jelenski, who edited and published them in *Kultura* in 1975.

Like *The marriage, Historia* takes the form of a dream. Like *Trans-Atlantyk*, but with a different focus, it has for its hero Gombrowicz himself. Act 1 takes place in his family home in Warsaw in 1914, where his parents and siblings express their disapproval of his associations with the lower class. In keeping with the dreamlike structure of *The marriage*, the characters then become school examiners and the Russian imperial family. The tsar (under whose rule most of Poland was at the time) entrusts Gombrowicz with a peace mission to Berlin. There he encounters William II and his confidant Prince Eulenburg (a departure from historical fact, since Eulenburg was disgraced after the 1905 scandal around his homosexuality). The following part is set in a literary café in Warsaw in the 1930s, involving fashionable poets and Marshal Pilsudski. The final section, which was to include Hitler and Stalin, was left unwritten. First staged in 1977 in Berlin, *Historia* has had several productions in Poland since.

Gombrowicz, ca. 1954–55 when staying with friends in Rosario, Argentina.

Rússovich moved out of the lodgings at 615 Venezuela to get married in September 1953. His wife Maria Rosa, a former employee of EAM Editions, had typed the French translation of *The marriage*. During the remainder of his stay in Argentina, Gombrowicz regularly visited Rússovich and his wife at the Rússovich family's estancia in Goya, in Corrientes Province. In March 1954, probably as a result of the mentions made of *Ferdydurke* in *Preuves*, Albert Camus wrote to Gombrowicz after reading his French version of *The marriage* and (so he claimed) most of *Ferdydurke* in Spanish. He saw little hope, he reported, to have the novel published in France, but he volunteered to share the text of the play with avant-garde directors of his acquaintance. Despite this show of support, *The marriage* had to wait another ten years to be performed.

In contrast with the shock caused by *Trans-Atlantyk*, the publication of the *Diary* by *Kultura*, in monthly installments, considerably improved Gombrowicz's standing with the Polish community in Buenos Aires, the largest in Latin America and matched in Europe only by those in Paris and London. Yet he remained a controversial figure, as was revealed at a public debate held on his work at the Polish Club in October 1954. By the fall of 1954, it became known that the Banco polaco was to be sold by the Polish government. When the news was confirmed in February 1955, Gombrowicz, fearing with good reason that his special status at the bank was unlikely to be honored by the new Argentinian owners, decided to leave his position, which he did in May. During the last six months, he supplemented his income by teaching evening courses in philosophy to groups of Polish women living

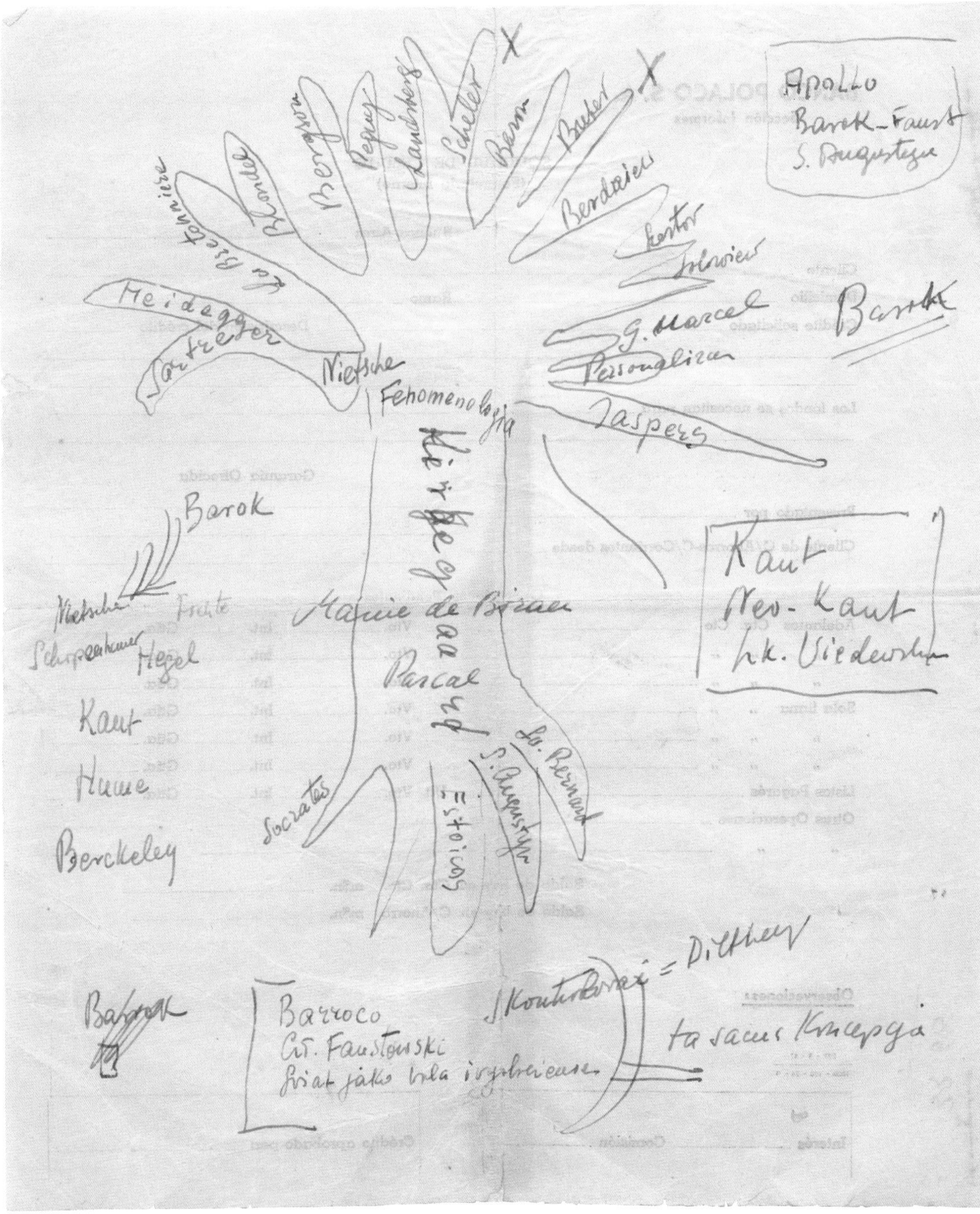

"The tree of philosophy."
Manuscript [ca. 1954–55].

in Buenos Aires. Most sessions were held at the home of his friend Maria Swieczewska. The Gombrowicz Archive preserves from these seminars a "philosophical tree" drawn by Gombrowicz: its four roots are Socrates, the Stoics, St. Augustine, and St. Bernard; the trunk is Pascal, Maine de Biran, Kierkegaard, Nietzsche, and phenomenology; the branches are about fifteen twentieth-century philosophers, including some unexpected names such as the French poet Charles Péguy. Also present in the archive are the notes Gombrowicz wrote on the philosophers he discussed. They are both in Polish and in Spanish and the philosophers covered are Descartes, Hegel, Heidegger, Husserl, Kant, Gabriel Marcel, Nietzsche, Sartre, Schelling, and Schopenhauer.

Gombrowicz's freedom from the Banco polaco—a liberation he greeted along with that of Argentina from Peronism in the same year—allowed him to devote himself exclusively to writing. He was able to obtain a small subvention from the American Committee for Free Europe. A certain liberalization also took place soon afterwards in Poland, in the aftermath of the "Thaw" that, in the Soviet Union, followed the admission of some of Stalin's crimes at the twentieth Congress of the Communist Party in 1956. Following demonstrations in Poznan in June, Wladyslaw Gomulka came to power in October 1956. The political liberalization allowed for the publication of authors hitherto banned officially or de facto. The availability of Gombrowicz's works in Poland consecrated his fame in his native country, making his name known to a new generation of readers. *Ferdydurke*, which had never been reprinted in Polish since the first edition twenty years before, was reissued in February 1957 by the Warsaw publisher PIW (Panstwowy Instytut Wydawniczy). A few changes were made by Gombrowicz to the text. The profoundly subversive character of *Ferdydurke* immediately found a new resonance in the context of Communist Poland, where ten thousand copies of this second edition were sold in a few days. In the words of Gombrowicz's future French translator Georges Sédir, who was in Poland at the time, it was as if "part of the youth spoke Gombrowiczian." Phrases such as the "rape through the ears," the famous passage at the end of the school episode when Kneadus whispers obscenities to Pylaszczkiewicz, were recycled politically to mean Stalinist propaganda.

Two more books by Gombrowicz came out in Poland in December 1957: *Trans-Atlantyk* and *The marriage*, in one volume, like the 1953 Kultura edition, issued by the Warsaw publishing house Czytelnik; and, under the title *Bakakaï*, a new, augmented edition of the stories published in 1933 as *Memories of the time of immaturity*. To the seven original tales, Gombrowicz added "In the service stair" (1929); the "Filidor" and "Filibert" tales incorporated in *Ferdydurke*; "The rat," written in 1937 and published in *Skamander* in 1939; and "The banquet," written in Buenos Aires after the war and published in 1953 in the London-based

Iwona, ksiezniczka Burgunda. Warsaw: Panstwowy Instytut Wydawniczy, 1958. Illustrated by Tadeusz Kantor. From the library of Witold Gombrowicz.

Polish émigré journal *Wiadomosci*. As for the title, Gombrowicz, perhaps still smarting from the derision the original one had met with, chose the name of the Buenos Aires street where he had lived in the early part of 1940, modifying its original spelling (Bacacay, after an Indian battle) as he had done for *Ferdydurke* with the name found in *Babbitt*. It was also in 1957 that plays by Gombrowicz were staged for the first time, when the Teatr Dramatyczny in Warsaw mounted *Iwona* on 29 November 1957, and the play had a run of performances until the end of February 1958. It was issued in book form by PIW later that year, with a dust-jacket and illustrations by Tadeusz Kantor. In the undated letter he wrote from Paris in reply to Gombrowicz's congratulations, the great Polish director declared himself eager to stage the play at his famous Cricot Theater in Cracow. He had not liked the Warsaw production, which he found too farcical. Kantor was not able to bring this plan to fruition. In May 1958, Gombrowicz learned from his brother Janusz that his works were about to be banned in Poland once more, as the short period of liberalization had come to an end. His books were not officially available in the country again until 1986. As for Kantor, many years later,

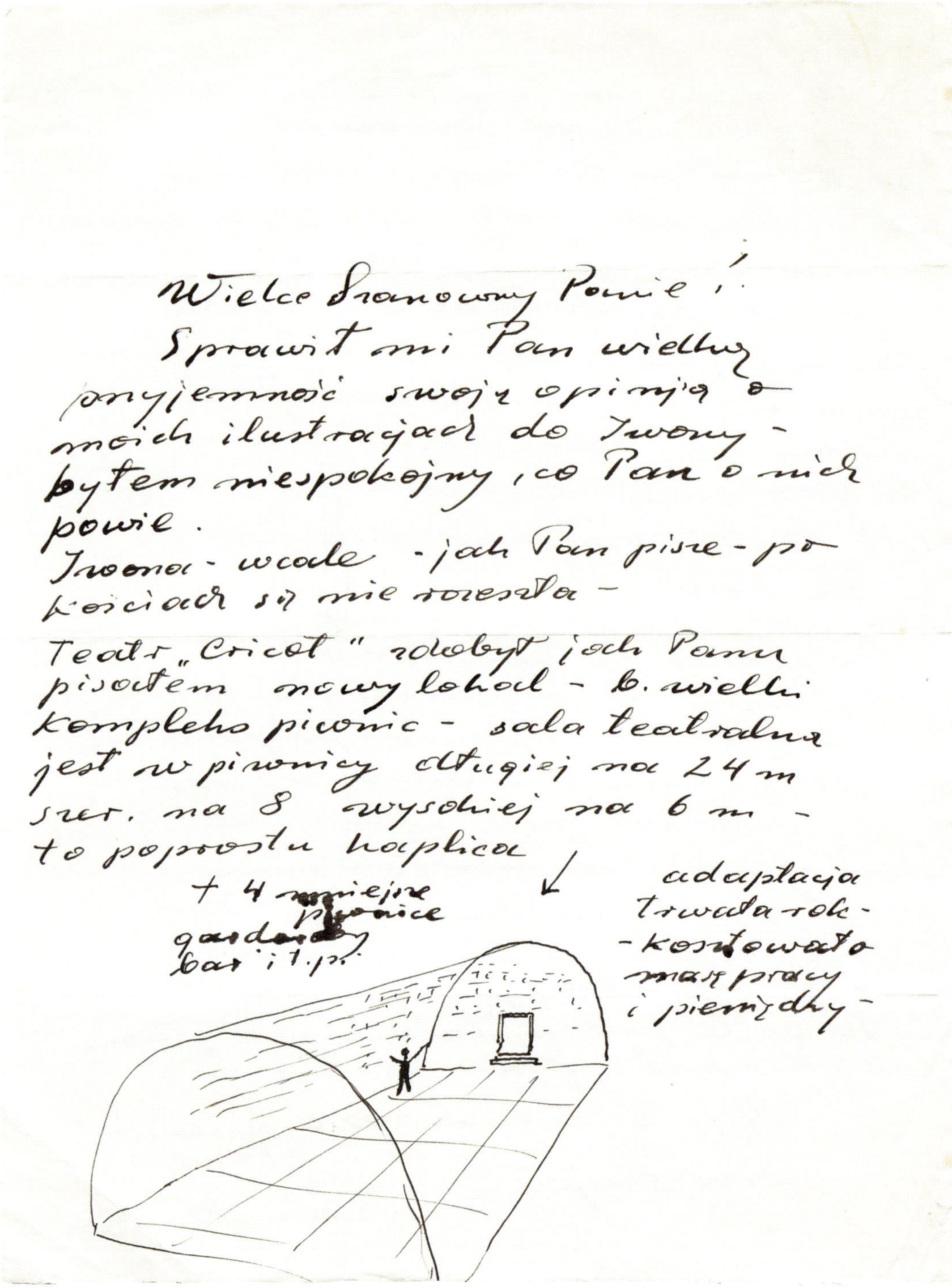

Wielce Szanowny Panie!
Sprawił mi Pan wielką
przyjemność swoją opinią o
moich ilustracjach do Iwony –
byłem niespokojny, co Pan o nich
powie.
Iwona – wcale – jak Pan pisze – po
kościach się nie rozeszła –
Teatr „Cricot" zdobył, jak Panu
pisałem nowy lokal – b. wielki
kompleks piwnic – sala teatralna
jest w piwnicy długiej na 24 m
szer. na 8 wysokiej na 6 m –
to poprostu kaplica

Tadeusz Kantor. Letter to Witold Gombrowicz, n.d. [1958].

in 1975, he adapted passages from *Ferdydurke* in the show that remains his most celebrated production, *The dead class*.

Meanwhile, the "Battle of Ferdydurke" was being successfully fought by Jelenski in Paris, as his correspondence with Gombrowicz shows. The latter had set out to translate the novel into French in May 1956, working from both the original Polish edition of 1937 (his battered, marked-up copy is preserved in the archive) and the Spanish version, in collaboration with Roland Martin, a young French journalist and translator then residing in Buenos Aires. Thanks to the support of the influential modernist literary critic Maurice Nadeau, this Gombrowicz-Martin translation was published in the fall of 1958 by René Julliard (who had declined the book two years before) in his series Les lettres nouvelles, while the first chapter appeared in the journal of the same title, which Nadeau edited. Prefaced by Jelenski, the translation was signed by the pseudonym "Brone," presented as "a French poet living in Buenos Aires"—a double mystification on the part of the author of "Contra los poetas," so contemptuous besides of the Argentinian intelligentsia's obsession with Paris and the French. Paradoxically, however—a paradox Gombrowicz was keenly aware of—it was the critical success of the book among the very same French intellectuals that launched his international career.

These important developments in the dissemination of his oeuvre coincided for Gombrowicz with a happy period in his life, despite the increasing attacks of asthma that eventually killed him. It was thus partly for medical reasons that, in October 1958, he paid the first of five extended visits to Tandil, a small, hilly city in the southeastern part of Buenos Aires Province. There, as he reported in his *Diary*, he became acquainted by chance with a group of literary and artistic-minded young Argentines in their early twenties who, also by chance, had discovered *Ferdydurke* in Spanish and fallen under its spell: Mariano Betelú, Jorge Di Paola, Juan Carlos Ferreyra, Juan Angel Magariños, Jorge Vilela. Together with other, younger friends from Buenos Aires, such as Juan Carlos Gómez and the writer Miguel Grinberg, who later edited the underground literary journal *Eco contemporaneo*, they formed a close support circle around the aging writer. Gombrowicz's Tandil friends admitted him, to quote Zofia Chadzynska's beautiful phrase, to "the citizenship of the young." Gombrowicz gave them nicknames: Betelú was thus "Guillé" or "Flor de Quilombo" (literally "flower of the bordello"), Ferreya "Fririri," Vilela "Marlon,"

Gombrowicz and his Tandil disciples, ca. 1958–60. Photo: Miguel Grinberg

and the very young Di Paola "Dipi" or "Asno" (ass). He encouraged their intellectual and artistic development, prefacing Di Paola's "dramatic poem" *Hernán* in 1963, or using Betelú's drawings to illustrate his works (such as the German edition of the *Diary*). As he noted wryly in his *Diary*, at that last stage in his Argentinian stay, he had found everything: readers, a literary café, disciples—except that the last were barely 20 years old.

In Tandil, Gombrowicz put the finishing touches on his novel *Pornografia*, his fourth, which he had begun in 1955, but drafted mostly in 1956–58. Published by the Instytut Literacki in 1960, it was soon translated into several European languages: the Italian translation appeared in the same year, followed by the French version in 1962—an outstanding achievement by the Polish writer Jerzy (Georges) Lisowski, who later became editor of the influential literary magazine *Twórczosc*—and the German one the following year. Before introducing this provocatively titled novel (Gombrowicz later deplored that the spread of commercial pornography made it sound banal), we should bear in mind Milosz's observation that Gombrowicz is unique in twentieth-century literature in that his oeuvre contains no description of the sexual act.

The story takes place, poignantly, in the early 1940s, in a Poland Gombrowicz never knew, and in Sandomir Province where he grew up. Like *Ferdydurke* and *Trans-Atlantyk*, it is a first-person narrative. The "Witold" of *Pornografia*, however, is closer to the philosophical I than to his real-life namesake, who could hardly have witnessed the events, purely imaginary in any case, chronicled in the novel. The main character is, rather, his Mephistophelian Doppelgänger, the mysterious Frederick, invited on the spirit of the moment by the narrator to accompany him on a visit to his friend Hippolytus. There, the two men notice an adolescent named Karol, whose spell on them does not come so much from his intrinsic beauty as from the fact that a radiant association is made in the minds of the two grown men between him and Henia, Hippolytus' daughter. Even though there is no involvement between Karol and Henia, the imaginations of Frederick and the narrator destine them erotically for each other. Seeing himself engaged in a feud against nature, the devilish, atheistic Frederick sets off a cruel psychological game involving Albert, Henia's older, respectable fiancé. The plot takes unexpected turns with the accidental killing of Albert's mother in a chance encounter with a young marauder; with open air rendez-vous between Henia and Karol "staged" by the voyeuristic Frederick; and, as the historical catalyst that precipitates the denouement, the arrival at Hippolytus' manor of an officer from the resistance who suddenly loses his nerves and whom Hippolytus and his friends are commanded to kill for fear he might betray others.

This extraordinarily dense, complex novel is built on themes of startling cruelty; yet it is told in a sober, elegant narrative whose grace is reminiscent of Stendhal, while the evocations of Ostrowiec and the park at Bodzechów have a poetic, haunting quality. The novel prolongs and adds serious touches to the dialogue initiated in *Ferdydurke* between maturity and immaturity, or adulthood and youth, while the historical background gives it a new urgency and humanity. Some readers—Czapski for one—resistant to the absurdist elements of the plays or left cold by the farcical, Pickwickian aspects of *Ferdydurke* have considered *Pornografia* Gombrowicz's masterpiece.

The publication of *Ferdydurke* in France, even if it was a critical rather than a popular success, had immediate repercussions in other European countries. The novel appeared in German in 1960, in English in 1961 (published in England by Macgibbon & Kee and in the United States by Harcourt Brace). A Dutch version followed in 1962, the work of Willem Maijer in collaboration with Herman van der Klei and Chris de Ruig, and an Italian translation the same year. These texts pose interesting bibliographical problems: Walter Tiel's German and the one in

Dutch were both prepared from the 1957 Polish edition; Eric Mosbacher and Sergio Minussi, on the other hand, based their English and Italian versions on the French text, which, as we have seen, derives both from the 1937 original and the 1947 Spanish edition. This practice of translating Gombrowicz from the French, which he himself sanctioned, was followed in other countries and for other works. As a result, a number of them were later retranslated. A problem of a different sort was the title of *Pornografia*, which was toned down in several languages: Tiel's first German translation was entitled *Verführung* (The seduction; the new, 1984 edition reverts to the title *Pornographie*). Similarly, the first Italian (1962) and Spanish (1965) versions were called, respectively, *La seduzione* and *La seducción*. Once again, Gombrowicz assented, commenting (in a characteristically patronizing way) that he understood that it might be embarrassing for some of his potential female readers to be overheard in a bookstore ordering a book entitled *Pornography*. Meanwhile, his work started appearing in major European literary journals, such as *Preuves* (whose editor François Bondy came to Buenos Aires to visit him in November 1960) or *Der Monat*. As for the *Diary*, the first volume came out in German in 1961, in French in 1964, and in Dutch in 1967 (but in English only in 1988).

Still, despite his growing international reputation, Gombrowicz's financial situation remained precarious. In the late 1950s and early 1960s, he accepted a commission from Radio Free Europe to prepare two series of autobiographical talks in Polish, one on Argentina, the other reminiscences of growing up in Poland before the war. These reminiscences were not broadcast. Discovered by Rita Gombrowicz in 1976 in a trunk of papers Gombrowicz had left in Argentina after his departure, they were published by the Instytut Literacki the following year as *Wedrówki po Argentynie* (Argentine peregrinations) and *Wspomnienia polskie* (Polish memories)—Gombrowicz's own titles. "Argentine peregrinations," written in 1958, and still unpublished in English, is an affectionate, if not uncritical portrait of Argentina, with picturesque accounts of its landscape and inhabitants. Given their intended audience, they are often based on comparisons, physical and moral, and including culinary habits, between Poles and Argentines (an all the more understandable approach given the size of the Polish émigré community in Argentina). The *Polish memories*, written subsequently, take Gombrowicz's life up to his return from Italy in 1938. They are an indispensable source of information on the author of *Ferdydurke*.

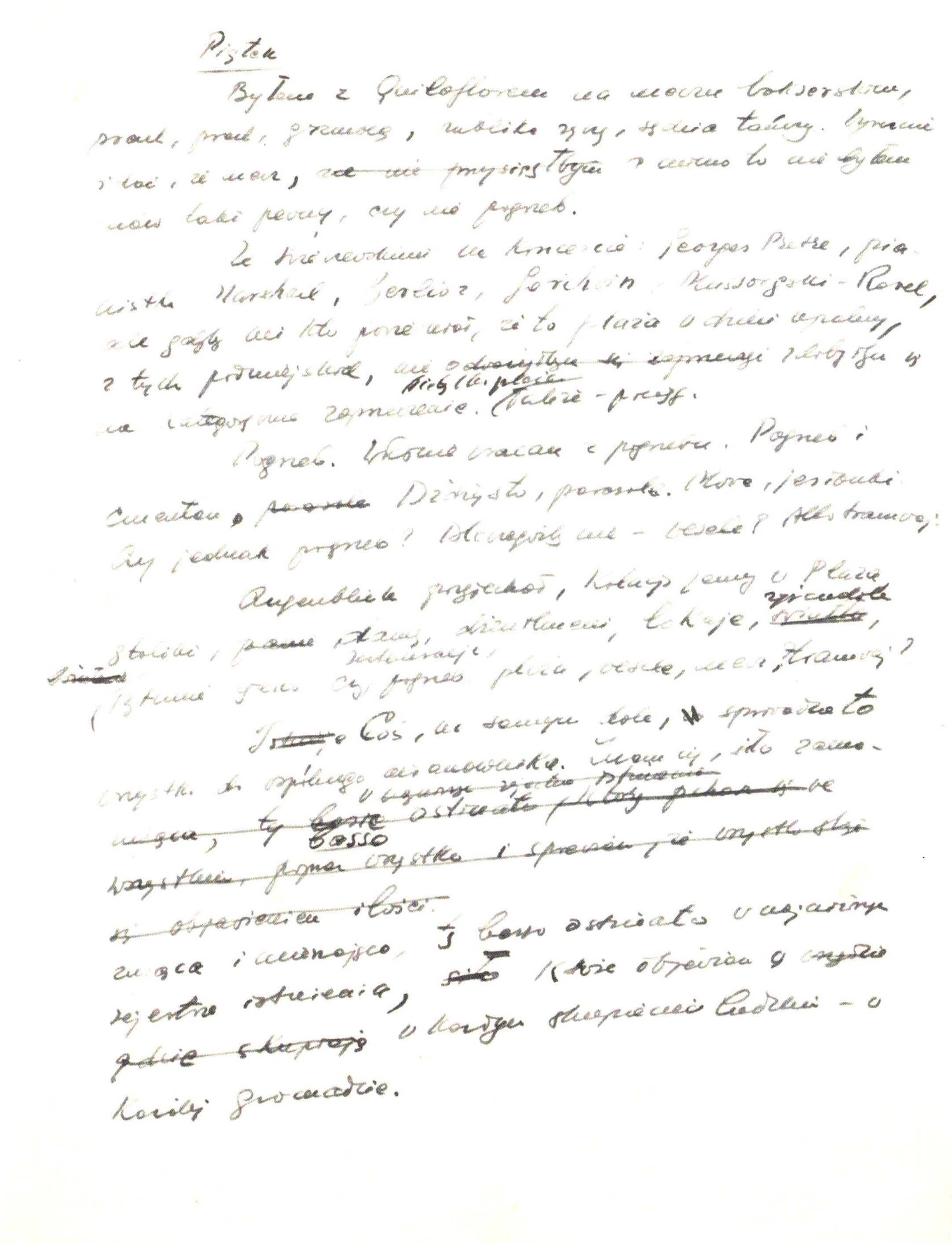

Diary for 1962, manuscript fragment.

Photograph of Gombrowicz and friends on 8 April 1963, the day he left Argentina.

Postcard photograph of the Federico Costa.

In the early 1960s, Gombrowicz was also recruited by the Buenos Aires publisher Jacobo Muchnik to collaborate in his *Diccionario de la literatura universal*, which eventually came out in 1967, by assisting with the entries on Polish authors. Another source of income was the $200 prize he received in 1961 from Kultura, which issued the second volume of his *Diary* (1957–61) the following year.

Gombrowicz, who had paid several visits to Uruguay in the preceding years, was in Piriapolis in February 1963 when he received from the Ford Foundation the opportunity to spend a year in Berlin on a fellowship. On 8 April 1963, after taking leave from Buenos Aires and Tandil friends, he sailed from Argentina on the *Federico Costa*. In a memorable passage of his *Diary*, he evokes the ghost of the *Chrobry* that had brought him to America twenty-three and a half years before.

From the exhibition:

Atlas général Larousse. Paris: Librairie Larousse, 1959. From the library of Witold Gombrowicz.

Mariano Lenogiry [i.e. Gombrowicz]. "El catolicismo frente a las nuevas corrientes en el arte." In *Criterio*, no. 831 (3 February 1944).

"Filidor forrado de nino." In *Papeles de Buenos Aires*, no. 3 (April 1944).

Photograph of the house at 615 Venezuela, Buenos Aires.

Ferdydurke, novela. Buenos Aires: Argos, 1947. From the library of Witold Gombrowicz.

Photograph of Virgilio Piñera in 1946.

Photograph of the Gran Rex café on Corrientes, Buenos Aires.

Photograph of the El Querandi café, on Perú at Moreno, Buenos Aires.

"Kronika Ferdydurke." Autograph notes, 1947.

Manuel Gálvez. Letter to Witold Gombrowicz, 31 July [1947?].

El casamiento. Buenos Aires: Ediciones EAM, 1948. From the library of Witold Gombrowicz.

Vastus Diccionario enciclopedico illustrado de la lingua castellana. Buenos Aires [1949]. 8th edition. From the library of Witold Gombrowicz.

"Contra los poetas." Typescript, with an autograph note, 1947.

Jaroslaw Iwaszkiewicz. Letter to Witold Gombrowicz, 28 January 1949.

9 Artes, no. 4 (Buenos Aires, April 1949). Contains "Cuatro respuestas de Witold Gombrowicz."

Józef Wittlin. Letter to Witold Gombrowicz, 9 January 1950 [i.e. 1951].

Martin Buber. Letter to Witold Gombrowicz, 9 July 1951.

Photograph of the president's room, Banco polaco, Buenos Aires.

Historia. Manuscript fragment of this unfinished play [1951].

Jerzy Giedroyc. Letter to Witold Gombrowicz, 13 April 1953.

François Bondy. "Note sur Ferdydurke." In *Preuves*, no. 32 (October 1953).

"The tree of philosophy." Manuscript [ca. 1954–55].

Manuscript notes on Husserl and Gabriel Marcel [ca. 1954–55].

Photograph of Gombrowicz, ca. 1954–55 when staying with friends in Rosario, Argentina.

Letter from Gombrowicz to Czeslaw Milosz, 15 February 1954.

Czeslaw Milosz. *Ziemia Ulro*, manuscript [ca. 1975].

Albert Camus. Letter to Witold Gombrowicz, 26 March 1954.

Photograph of Gombrowicz and Alejandro Rússovich, ca. 1954–55.

Trans-Atlantyk — Slub. Z komentarzem autora. Warsaw: Czytelnik, 1957. From the library of Witold Gombrowicz.

Iwona, ksiezniczka Burgunda. Warsaw: Panstwowy Instytut Wydawniczy, 1958. Illustrated by Tadeusz Kantor. From the library of Witold Gombrowicz.

Program and photographs from the first production of *Iwona, ksiezniczka Burgunda* on 29 September 1957 at the Teatr Dramatyczny, from *Teatr Dramatyczny w Warszawie* (Warsaw: Panstwowe Wydawnictwo Naukowe, 1972).

Tadeusz Kantor. Letter to Witold Gombrowicz, n.d. [1958].

Constantin Jelenski. Letter to Witold Gombrowicz, 10 January 1958.

"Le rapt." In *Les lettres nouvelles*, no. 68 (November 1958).

Photograph of Gombrowicz and his Tandil disciples, ca. 1958–60.

Virgilio Piñera. Letter to Witold Gombrowicz, 3 February 1959.

Gombrowicz photographed by Maria Swieczewska on board the *Costanera*, on the Rio de la Plata, ca. 1960.

Das Tagebuch des Witold Gombrowicz. [German translation by Walter Tiel] Pfullingen: Neske, 1961.

Diary for 1962, manuscript fragment.

Ferdydurke. Prefazione di Angelo M. Ripellino. Turin: Giulio Einaudi editore, 1961 (1966 printing).

Pornografia. Milan: Bompiani, 1962, 1972 ed. (I più famosi libri moderni, no. 257).

Ferdydurke. Paris: Union générale d'éditions, 1964 (collection 10/18).

Jorge Di Paola Levin. "Gombrowicz de Polonia: Ferdydurke de sí mismo." In *ECO contemporaneo*, no. 5 (1963).

"La forma que nos deforma." In *ECO contemporaneo*, no. 8/9 (Winter 1965).

"Diario argentino." In *ECO contemporaneo*, no. 10 (Winter 1967).

Moritz von Bomhard. Letter to Witold Gombrowicz, 13 March 1963.

Photograph of Gombrowicz and friends on 8 April 1963, the day he left Argentina.

Postcard photograph of the *Federico Costa*.

Vitold Gombrowicz à Paris

Polonais émigré en Argentine, Vitold Gombrowicz est de passage à Paris. Nous avons demandé à Piotr Rawicz, l'auteur très remarqué du Sang du ciel, *et lui aussi émigré de l'Europe de l'Est, de nous présenter cet écrivain dont la réputation commence à devenir mondiale.*

« *Le « je » et le « moi », voici les deux mots les plus importants du langage humain* », lance Gombrowicz, et la formulation lapidaire de cet impérialisme, de cet expansionnisme hors pair d'un « ego » créateur, qui se veut et se connaît souverain, paraîtrait irritante, n'était l'orgueil de bon aloi, n'était la présence de l'homme, n'était derrière et à l'appui du personnage l'une des œuvres littéraires les plus insolites et, jusqu'à un passé tout récent, les plus injustement méconnues de l'époque. L'injustice commence d'ailleurs à être réparée grâce aux dernières assises de la littérature internationales à Corfou, dont ce poète polonais fut une des vedettes.

C'est en France qu'avec la publication en 1958 par Julliard de l'inoubliable *Ferdydurke* (et, en 1962, de *la Pornographie*) s'est mise à poindre la gloire tardive et tant méritée de Gombrowicz ; cette gloire qui, grâce à une dizaine de traductions, tend à présent à gagner des pays nouveaux. Ce ne sera pas, je le crains, une implantation rapide, en raison du « splendide isolement » de l'œuvre et de l'auteur parmi les courants de l'époque. Toutefois, là où l'œuvre réussira à s'imposer son succès n'aura rien d'éphémère. Il y a déjà à présent, de par le monde, de petits groupes d' « initiés », de fervents de Gombrowicz (comme ça été le cas pour un Joyce ou pour un Malcolm Lowry), une sorte de franc-maçonnerie gombrowiczienne qui compte en France, par exemple, des écrivains comme René de Obaldia. Une seule exception à ce caractère jusqu'à présent « caméral » de l'audience du poète : la Pologne, son pays d'origine : « *Lorsque, à la faveur du « dégel », le gouvernement polonais autorisa en* 1957 *la réimpression de* Ferdydurke *(paru pour la première fois à Varsovie en* 1937) *puis de mes autres livres, le succès en fut tel* — se plaint l'écrivain — *qu'après un certain temps je fus de nouveau interdit...* »

Un splendide isolement

Mais, tout d'abord, qui est Gombrowicz, où situer l'homme et le poète ? La biographie nous aidera à peine à saisir ce phénomène bizarre, unique et puissant. Avant la guerre un recueil de nouvelles, *Bakakai*, et ensuite le roman *Ferdydurke*. En 1939 il s'établit en Argentine, où il vit à peu près inconnu en écrivant entre autres les romans *Trans-Atlantique* et *la Pornographie*, ceci sans parler d'un *Journal* en plusieurs volumes auquel il continue de travailler parallèlement à son œuvre romanesque et théâtrale (1). Une de ses pièces, *le Mariage*, sera montée à Paris en juin. Après une absence d'un quart de siècle il vient d'arriver en Europe, et le voici happé, un peu écrasé et scandalisé par le mécanisme de sa célébrité naissante : interviews, réceptions, réunions, rencontres...

Non point que Gombrowicz soit un timide, « *mais en Argentine*, explique-t-il, *je vivais en dehors des milieux « culturels », entouré uniquement d'amis dont le plus âgé n'avait pas plus de vingt-cinq ans. C'est avec eux que j'ai pris l'habitude d'élaborer ma « politique littéraire », un mélange de provocation, de jeu, de bêtise, de bizarrerie, d'indolence... Bref l'univers de la jeunesse.* »

Le voici mis face à face avec la « foire », avec la « pléthore » parisienne... « *Quarante mille peintres dans cette ville*, dit Gombrowicz, *dont quatre à peine sont authenthiques. Des milliers d'écrivains ou qui se considèrent comme tels. La bêtise, l'imposture, conscientes ou inconscientes, ont atteint leurs limites. Le scandale ne durera pas.* »

Dans sa bouche, cet aristocratisme hautain, ce souci de qualité et d'authenticité n'ont rien d'artificiel.

J'essaie pourtant de cerner le phénomène Gombrowicz, de le situer du moins par rapport à la géographie et à l'histoire. Je lui parle de ses deux grands contemporains polonais : Bruno Schulz, une sorte de Kafka (en plus « lyrique ») assassiné par les nazis et dont le *Traité des mannequins* publié récemment par Julliard marque à mon sens une date ; de Witkiewicz (qui s'est suicidé en 1939 en Pologne) dont *l'Inassouvissement* (un incroyable roman d'anticipation sur l'avènement du communisme chinois, publié en 1929) attend toujours en France une équipe de traducteurs « congéniaux » et un éditeur courageux... Gombrowicz se défend avec acharnement et non sans raison contre ce terme de « grande triade polonaise » où je serais tenté de l'emprisonner et où je mets, à l'entendre, deux noms de trop... Rien de plus éloigné, en effet, de son monde sec, hyperlucide, férocement discipliné, que l'univers « kafkaïen » (nous détestons tous deux cet adjectif barbare) d'un Schulz ou que la puissance torrentielle, prophétique, débordante, d'un Witkiewicz.

Lorsque je lui fais remarquer que la destruction, la pulvérisation créatrice et révolutionnaire du langage dans *Ferdydurke* (je parle du texte polonais) fait de lui, du moins dans ce domaine, un précurseur d'Ionesco, il trouve la chose plausible mais secondaire. Il ne connaît pas encore l'œuvre de René de Obaldia où pourtant il trouverait des éléments d'un paysage familier. Il aime Montaigne, Rabelais, Jarry et Gide, mais pas du tout Proust. Il admire Sartre comme philosophe et considère que « *les Français ont raté une grande occasion, n'ayant pas assimilé comme il convenait* l'Etre et le Néant ». Pour guider les lecteurs français vers des régions tant soit peu familières, je mentionnerai le Queneau de l'époque du *Chiendent*. Mais Gombrowicz serait-il prêt à admettre seulement un voisinage quel qu'il soit ?

« *Je suis un vieux campagnard, un peu méfiant et froid*, dit-il. *Je me méfie des concepts et mon œuvre est la satire de la conceptualisation. Je me suis défini, une fois, comme une aspirine, car je sers le relâchement... Mon art est le contraire du « nouveau roman » français qui se veut descriptif et objectif. Je ne me soumets pas à l'objet, moi. Je veux séduire les gens, je cherche la supériorité, la domination, l'expansion de mon « moi ». Ce n'est point là une philosophie, mais l'attitude pratique d'un artiste... L'homme est en conflit perpétuel avec la forme, quelle qu'elle soit. La parodie est sa vengeance...*

« Amoureux de l'immaturité »

» *Mon drame personnel découle de deux sources*, ajoute Gombrowicz, *une dégradation vengeresse de toute forme, et puis... ma soumission humiliante à la jeunesse. En tant qu'artiste cherchant la perfection, je tends vers la maturité et en même temps je suis follement amoureux de l'immaturité, de l'inachevé. La solution n'existe pas, ne peut pas exister, car si je deviens mûr je cesse d'être jeune et ainsi de suite...* »

***

Voici donc évoqué par lui-même le thème central de l'œuvre de Gombrowicz : l'immaturité. Mais cet écrivain doué d'une intelligence prodigieuse, ce poète qui à aucun prix — il y insiste — ne veut passer ni pour un philosophe ni pour un théoricien, est-il semblable à l'image qu'il trace de lui ? Il se veut « aspirine », relâchement, et il est tension. Entre cette maturité douloureusement tendue vers la jeunesse et cette jeunesse tendue vers la maturité, il évolue nécessairement dans un climat philosophique, voire didactique, qu'il déteste. Ce n'est pas un hasard si dans son œuvre apparaît sporadiquement l'obsession cauchemardesque des professeurs, de l'école, semblable à une pompe aspirante qui « cuculise » les adultes s'aventurant dans son orbite. Entre la tentative et son aboutissement (qui est toujours son échec), entre la forme et ce qu'elle est censée cerner ou contenir, entre l'expression et son objet, il y a, nous le savons tous, un hiatus, un décalage, un terrain vague. Gombrowicz est à mon sens le poète cruellement précis de ce terrain vague. C'est là sa grandeur et son drame, le drame d'un « formaliste » qui raille les formes, d'un réaliste qui non seulement entrevoit mais qui vit charnellement l'inconsistance fatale, la pluralité douloureuse de ce qu'on appelle communément « réalité ».

Il ne veut pas convaincre, mais séduire. Y est-il parvenu ? Je l'avoue : son univers superbe, puissamment charpenté, n'est pas sans m'effrayer. Il ne me paraît humecté d'aucune goutte de pitié.

PIOTR RAWICZ.

(1) Le premier tome du *Journal* paraîtra prochainement chez Julliard dans la collection « Lettres nouvelles ».

CHAPTER THREE

Paris-Berlin-Vence, 1963–69

After a short stop in Barcelona, the *Federico Costa* docked at Cannes on 22 April 1963. The next day, Gombrowicz was in Paris, where he spent three weeks until his departure for Berlin. In his *Diary*, he gave a rather satirical account of this stay in the French capital to match his earlier pronouncements questioning the traditional admiration for French models. It was in Paris, to be sure, that some of his strongest allies, on the Polish as well as on the French side, were established: Jelenski, whom he met in person for the first time; Bondy; Giedroyc and his Kultura colleagues; Nadeau, who had imposed *Ferdydurke* on an originally reluctant publisher, and his close collaborator Geneviève Serreau; not to mention the many admirers Gombrowicz's novel had found within French intellectual circles. It is a measure of the esteem in which he was held (and of Jelenski's genius as an impresario) that his short visit was covered by *Le Monde*, in the form of an interview with the Polish-born writer and journalist Piotr Rawicz (an Auschwitz survivor, whose novel *Blood from the sky* was published in French in 1961). Yet it was more important, from Gombrowicz's standpoint, to present his relationship to Paris in a contentious mode. In the *Diary*, Paris is disparaged as a place of self-confident maturity, its poetic charm inspiring in Gombrowicz as much suspicion as poetry in general, while a visit to the Louvre with Hector Bianciotti, the Argentinian-born French writer, is a pretext for a tirade against art. French literature was then dominated by the Nouveau Roman, some of whose practitioners greatly admired Gombrowicz's works, but the least one can say is that this admiration was not reciprocated. Two figures escaped Gombrowicz's contempt, though he does not appear to have had any personal contact with either: Jean-Paul Sartre, whose *L'être et le néant* he held in high esteem (but whose huge *Critique de la raison dialectique*, of 1960, he abandoned after 168 pages, on the evidence of the copy in his library); and Jean Genet, whose theater is not without analogy with his own, and whom he considered the most significant French writer active at the time.

Piotr Rawicz. "Vitold Gombrowicz à Paris." From *Le Monde* for 18 May 1963.

An important encounter took place in early May at the Café de la Paix in Paris between Gombrowicz and the young Argentinian director Jorge Lavelli. Born in 1934, Lavelli had moved to France in 1960 and was about to enter the competition for young theatrical troupes sponsored by the French Ministry of Foreign

Affairs with the first authorized production of *The marriage* and the first outside Poland. According to his later testimony to Rita Gombrowicz, Lavelli had discovered the play in the Rússovich translation when he was still in Argentina. While this Spanish version remained unperformed, the original Polish was staged for the first time in 1960 by the student troupe of the Gliwice Polytechnic Institute. It was directed by Jerzy Jarocki, with sets and costumes by the young designer Krystyna Zachwatowicz, wife of the film director Andrzej Wajda. Since Gombrowicz was banned from publication in his native country, the four performances were given without the author's name. Having moved to Paris in the early 1960s, Zachwatowicz brought the play to Lavelli's attention. Dissatisfied with the French translation prepared in Argentina under the author's supervision, they commissioned a new one from Jadwiga Kukulczanska and Georges Sédir. (Kukulczanska used the delightful, Gombrowiczian nom-de-plume Koukou Chanska, which Gombrowicz pronounced "rather strange" in the *Diary*; she and Sédir went on to translate other works by Gombrowicz). Having won the prize in June 1963, Lavelli was able to present *The marriage* at the Théâtre Récamier in Paris in January 1964. After a tumultuous dress rehearsal on 7 January, the play opened to reviews that ranged from the enthusiastic (Guy Dumur in *France-Observateur* referred to it as "total theater") to the indignant. A devastating one came from Gabriel Marcel, one of the philosophers covered in Gombrowicz's courses in Buenos Aires.

Lavelli's production revealed Gombrowicz as a playwright of the stature of Beckett and Genet; it also made the Argentinian director famous. He treated the text of *The marriage* like a musical composition, the deliberately non-realistic delivery reflecting the play's dream-like atmosphere. The stage music, which was given an important role, was the work of the avant-garde composer Diego Masson (son of the surrealist painter André Masson). It was written for two percussionists, one of them the composer himself; alternating as the other were Jean-Pierre Drouet, recognized since as one of the finest French percussionists of his generation, and Jean-Claude Casadesus, also at the dawn of his career as a leading French conductor. Several members of the cast later testified that those performances were among the highest points in their careers. Disconcerted by some of Gombrowicz's comments at their meeting, Lavelli had discouraged him from attending the rehearsals; he was, in turn, disappointed that the playwright, then in Germany, could not see a performance. After its initial run at the Récamier, Lavelli's production of *The marriage* was presented in several other venues. It was seen for the last time at the Berlin Festival in January 1965. The film made on that occasion is preserved in the Gombrowicz Archive. In that year 1965, Lavelli directed *Yvonne, princess of Burgundy* with (appropriately) the Théâtre de Bourgogne. This production was first seen at the Venice Festival, then in Paris, Zurich, and Buenos Aires. After Gombrowicz's death, Lavelli also directed his last play, *Operetta*.

Gombrowicz was invited to Berlin, as a writer in residence, at Bondy's and Jelenski's instigation, as part of a vast program established under the auspices of the Ford Foundation in order to promote the cultural life of the former German capital and save it from the isolation that threatened it after the erection of the Wall in August 1961. This ambitious project was the brainchild of the composer Nicolas Nabokov, then cultural adviser to the mayor of Berlin, but who also had close ties with the Congress for Cultural Freedom, with which Jelenski and Bondy were associated. On his arrival on 16 May, Gombrowicz was first housed at the Akademie der Künste; he then moved to a hotel on the Kurfürstendamm, before settling in a drab, noisy two-room apartment on Hohenzollerndamm, where he remained until 1 November 1963. During the last six months, he occupied a studio at the top of a modern building in the Tiergarten area, but he also spent several weeks in a clinic. Throughout his stay in Germany, Gombrowicz was beset with health troubles, from mild heart problems to a bout of influenza that his asthma made worse. He was also suffering from depression and missed Argentina and the friends he had left behind. In a moving episode of his *Berlin Diary*, he evokes a walk in the Tiergarten during which the smell of the grass, water, and trees reminded him of the Poland of his childhood, a short train ride away, while making him realize that his return to Europe was also a journey toward death.

Gombrowicz's fellow Ford Foundation invitees included the Austrian poet Ingeborg Bachman, the Brazilian sculptor Mario Cravo, the American painter Shirley Jaffé, the English writer Pier Paul Read, the Greek-French composer and architect Iannis Xenakis. The French Nouveau Roman writer Michel Butor, whom Gombrowicz had previously met in Argentina, subsequently joined the group. The *Berlin Diary* also relates, in a humorous, distorted fashion, the contacts Gombrowicz had with prominent

German writers, such as Günter Grass, whose *Tin Drum* (1958) and more recent *Katz und Maus* had had a phenomenal success; the young Uwe Johnson, whose novel *Das dritte Buch über Achim* had been awarded the Formentor Prize in 1962; and the left-wing playwright Peter Weiss. They all have left their own accounts of Gombrowicz in Berlin, Grass's and Weiss's generally sympathetic, Johnson's not so.

Rather than cultivating the German literary élite, Gombrowicz tried to recreate in Berlin the kind of artistic and literary café he had patronized in Warsaw in the mid to late 1930s and, even more assiduously, in Buenos Aires throughout his Argentinian exile. From late August until January 1964, he held sessions, co-hosted with Helmut Jaesrich, the editor of *Der Monat*, at the Café Zuntz on the Kurfürstendamm. A qualified success, this experiment nevertheless allowed Gombrowicz to make contacts with younger intellectuals of both sexes who admired him, such as the pianist Lissa Bauer, the painter Eva Bechman, the theatrical photographer Susanna Fels, the art critic Christos Joachimides, Tadeusz Kulik, a Polish student, or the lawyer Otto Schily. In July 1963, Gombrowicz gave a public reading, followed by questions, before an international student audience. Organized by Walter Höllerer, the head of the Berlin Literarisches Colloquium, this *Lesung* was highly successful, even though Gombrowicz's account of it in the *Berlin Diary* is characteristically ironical.

While Gombrowicz was in Berlin, a press campaign was launched against him in Poland in response to an article he published in German, in August 1963 in the magazine *Akzente*, to protest new restrictions on intellectual freedom. The campaign took the form of articles denouncing his so-called anti-Polish tendencies, published in Warsaw in the newly founded journal *Kultura* (the Communist answer to the Paris-based monthly) and in Cracow in *Zycie literackie* (The literary life). This campaign, which prompted rejoinders from Gombrowicz's friends in the émigré press in Paris and London, chiefly targeted Gombrowicz's presence in Berlin. It is to be understood within the larger context of the political tensions of the year 1963, in which the status of West Berlin played a major part. Even the Polish critic Artur Sandauer, who had praised and popularized Gombrowicz's work in the 1950s (the archive contains a substantial correspondence that continued until 1968), was pressured into joining the fray with an ideologically oriented critique of *Pornografia*; he also hinted at Gombrowicz's purported fascist tendencies, basing this denunciation on a montage of quotations from the *Diary*, a work banned in Poland until 1986 (when it was published with 17 lines of cuts). This campaign against him greatly affected Gombrowicz, as did attacks regularly emanating from the London-based Polish émigré journal *Wiadomosci*.

Royaumont.
Photo: Rita Gombrowicz

Gombrowicz left Berlin for Paris on 17 May 1964. Welcomed at Orly by Jelenski and his own nephew Józef Gombrowicz, son of his brother Janusz, he spent his first few days at the house of Kultura in Maisons-Laffitte. During the following three months, he was a fellow at the Cercle culturel de Royaumont, an international cultural center then operated by the Gouïn-Lang Foundation at the partly ruined Cistercian abbey located about twenty miles north of Paris. Once again, Gombrowicz found himself in the Parisian intellectual climate he so disliked—a feeling no doubt exacerbated by the refusal of many "serious" French intellectuals at the time to see anything wrong with the Communist regimes of Eastern Europe. Accordingly, as he charmingly put it to the visiting Polish writer Janusz Odrowaz-Pienazek, he took his revenge by constantly "putting his stick into the anthill." The ferocious account he gave of this stay at Royaumont in his *Diary* leaves out the most important biographical element: his meeting with a young doctoral student from Montreal, Marie-Rita Labrosse, who became the companion of his last years.

Mariano Betelú at La Plata in 1965.

Until the summer of 1964, Gombrowicz still retained hopes of returning to Argentina, a country he had come to love so much that it had become a second home or, to borrow the neologism of *Trans-Atlantyk*, his "filistria," and where he had made plans to settle in La Plata with Betelú and Gómez. In that same year 1964, the Piñera translation of *Ferdydurke* was reissued in Buenos Aires by Editorial Sudamerica, with a new preface by Ernesto Sábato. (Four years later, the same firm published the Spanish translation of Gombrowicz's *Diary* up to 1963 under the title *Diario argentino*.) Gombrowicz reciprocated three years later by prefacing the French translation of Sábato's novel *Sobre héroes y tumbas*. He was aware of no book, he claimed, "that is a better introduction to the secrets of Latin American sensibility, its myths, phobias, and fascinations."

In late October 1964, after a few weeks in Cabris, near Grasse, Gombrowicz and Rita Labrosse settled in a rented flat on the third floor of a large Art Nouveau house, the Villa Alexandrine, in the picturesque hillside town of Vence, above Nice. There he was to spend his five remaining years, which his wife has movingly

The Villa Alexandrine in Vence.
Photo: Leprince

Illustration by Jan Lebenstein for "Événements sur la goélette Banbury." In *Preuves*, nos. 147 and 148 (May–June 1963).

chronicled in the memoir that forms the final chapter of her *Gombrowicz en Europe*.

Cosmos, Gombrowicz's last novel, was begun in Buenos Aires in February 1961, continued in Berlin in 1963–64, and completed in Vence in early December 1964. It is the only Gombrowicz novel preserved in manuscript in his archive in its various versions, of which there are five, not counting corrected proofs. An additional draft, also preserved in the Beinecke Library, turned up in the papers of Jelenski, one of the book's first readers, whose enthusiastic reaction, in a letter dated June 1965, is also in the archive. An early state of the opening chapter was published in 1962 in *Kultura*, which issued the whole novel in September 1965. Both the French translation (by Georges Sédir) and the German version (by Walter Tiel, entitled *Indizien*) appeared in 1966: Eric Mosbacher's English text, which came out in 1967, is derived not from the Polish but from these French and German versions.

Gombrowicz had published in 1938, in the Warsaw journal *Czas*, a short essay entitled "The misfortunes of Zakopane," which gave a satirical portrait of this small resort in the Tatra Mountains, to the south of Cracow, which he visited often in the 1930s. Zakopane serves as the background of *Cosmos*. The most "austere" of Gombrowicz's works by his own admission, *Cosmos* seems to be the realization of Flaubert's dream of writing a novel on the theme of nothing. It is not that nothing happens in the book, which culminates, in fact, in a dramatic incident: the suicide by hanging of an innocuous young man during a group excursion in the surroundings of Zakopane. That death is ultimately left unexplained, or, it can also be argued, over-explained by a multitude of small signs that precede it, beginning, in the first chapter, with the discovery by the narrator (a young student by the name of Witold) and his friend Fuks of a dead sparrow hanging by a wire in a clump of trees. This happening, at once bizarre and banal, leads Witold and his friend to a detective-like investigation of the inhabitants of the house where they rent a room: Leon Wojtys, a retired bank director; his wife; their daughter Lena; her husband Ludwik; their maid Katasia, whose upper lip was damaged in a car accident. The narrator's imagination collects signs from the most concrete occurrences and tries to associate and interpret them like constellations in the sky (hence the novel's title). Caught in his own game, he inserts in the plot a red herring of his own when, in a gratuitous act, he strangles and hangs Lena's cat, in a scene that recalls other instances of

Witold Gombrowicz

KOSMOS

(początek powieści, będącej w opracowaniu)

Dłoga piaszczysta, gorąco drgające, czarne drzewa ~~iglaste~~ ~~wdzierające się~~ między domki, płoty, pola ciemne pod słońcem ~~sięgające~~ aż po las, my zaś idziemy ~~drogą w przejrzystym~~ upale. Pot. Idzie Tun, ja za nim wlokę się i patrzę ~~na jego~~ nogawki, obcasy włażą w piach. Idziemy, idziemy, idziemy, patrzę w dół, ziemia, koleiny drogi, piasek i gruda, błyski z dołu, ze szklistych kamyków, górą blask, brzęczenie nieruchome upału. Skwar. Mnie wtedy do trzydziestki ze dwóch lat brakowało, aplikantem byłem w sądzie, ale prawo juz coraz bardziej mi brzydło i zaczynałem flirty z literaturą. Pojechałem w lecie do pewnej miejscowości na podkarpaciu zeby się mimo wszystko do egzminu adwokackiego przygotować, ale nie wiedziałem gdzie zamieszkać, bo wskazany mi pensjonat był jeszcze zamknięty - przypadkiem na ulicy spotkałem Tuna - ~~Tun~~ widywałem go często za szkolnych czasów, ale potem przestałem widywać i nie powiem zeby mnie entuzjazmem wypełniła jego ryże, ~~ślamazarne~~ oblicze jasno blond wyłupiaste ze spojrzeniem ~~jak~~ wysmarowanym apatią. Ale okazało się, ze tez poszukuje pokoju, tudziez ze ma adres dworku, gdzie i taniej, bo daleko, na samym wylocie - i właśnie tam szedł, zostawiwszy rzeczy w hotelu przy stacji, więc i ja z nim się wybrałem, zostawiwszy rzeczy, bo jednak wolałem z nim niz w pojedynkę. Idziemy tedy, nogawki jego przedemną, wraz z obcasami, droga i gorąc, patrzę w dół, ziemia i piach, iskrzą się kamyczki, raz, dwa, raz, dwa, nogawki i obcasy, pot i śpik, z oczu niewyspanych powoli wszystko straciłem oprócz kroczenia tego oddolnego. Stanął.

1

Kosmos. Opening page, typescript, corrected [ca. 1961].

Witold and Rita Gombrowicz with their dog Psina in their Citroën 2-CV, Vence, 1967.
Photo: Bohdan Paczowski

Gombrowicz at his desk at the Villa Alexandrine in Vence.
Photo: Bohdan Paczowski

suffering inflicted on animals in Gombrowicz's works. (As the readers of his *Diary* know from many memorable passages, Gombrowicz loved animals and had a deep horror of their suffering; in Vence, he and Rita Labrosse adopted a dog whom he named Psina, the Polish for "doggie.") This macabre episode leads to Leon's proposal of an excursion in the mountains, in the company of two other young couples and a priest they meet on the way. The excursion, in turn, leads to one of the book's most virtuoso episodes, in which Leon introduces the narrator into his private world, a revelation that is both biographical—the purpose of the excursion turns out to be to commemorate a sexual encounter he had there with the female cook of the mountain hut—and linguistic—his delight in using the nonsense word "berg." Is "berg" a reference to the mountains, a Jewish joke, a coded allusion to an old school joke? Gombrowicz never explained it.

While Gombrowicz's works remained officially inaccessible in Poland, the last years of his life saw his celebrity grow on both sides of the Atlantic. Following the success of Lavelli's productions of *The marriage* and *Iwona,* his plays were performed in several European countries. In November 1964, he received a letter from Ingmar Bergman in which the Swedish film director conveyed his admiration for *Iwona* and indicated that he intended to stage it in Stockholm. This project came to fruition three decades later, when Bergman chose Gombrowicz's play to mark what was announced at the time as his retirement from the theater. Another prominent Swedish director, Alf Sjöberg (1903–80), mounted *Iwona* at the Royal Swedish Theater in November 1965. Sjöberg

From the Sjöberg production of *The marriage.*

went on to direct *The marriage* with even greater success in December 1966. The third major production of the play in Gombrowicz's lifetime was by Ernst Schröder at the Schiller-Theater in West Berlin, with Helmut Griem as Henryk and Schröder himself as the Father. During the Vence years, Gombrowicz saw a performance of one of his plays for the first and only time, when the young company of Bernard Fontaine mounted *Yvonne, princesse de Bourgogne* at the Centre culturel méditerranéen in Nice in December 1967. The playwright was so moved by the occasion that it triggered an attack of asthma. To his disappointment, however, no theater during his lifetime attempted to stage his new play, *Operetta,* which he considered his most accessible work.

Program of Alf Sjöberg production of *Yvonne, prinsessa av Bourgogne,* at the Dramatiska Teatern (Stockholm, Sweden), 1966.

The last of Gombrowicz's plays, *Operetta* is also the one that took him the longest to write. Having left unfinished the original version, *Historia,* in 1955, he began on an entirely new basis (having written *Pornografia* in the meantime) during his first Tandil stay in 1958. This new draft was revised twice in the following years, as shown by the various versions, especially of the last two acts, preserved in the archive. The play was put aside once again while Gombrowicz worked on *Cosmos,* to be resumed in Vence at the end of 1964 and completed in 1966. Published in Polish the following year, it was immediately translated into French, while appearing in Italian and in Swedish in 1968. Gombrowicz had originally reserved the rights to the premiere for Alf Sjöberg, but the Swedish director declined to mount it for ideological reasons. He was evidently ill at ease with the play's mockery of Marxist rhetoric and political ambiguity (the left-wing intellectual is a self-hating professor afflicted with perpetual nausea). The playwright's correspondence with Sjöberg reveals how profoundly hurt and disappointed he was by this display of what was not yet called political correctness.

Operetta is, to be sure, the most overtly political of Gombrowicz's three completed plays. This political dimension contrasts with the traditional frivolity of the form. The fact that *Operetta* has been promoted from subtitle to title seems to suggest that Gombrowicz is attempting to capture the essence of a genre, in the manner of Ravel writing *La valse*. The play, however, is not so much a homage to operetta as its parody. The play is set before 1914 (like *Historia*) in the never-never-land principality of Himalay. The prince's son, Count Charmant, and his "double" Baron Firulet, two fops on the verge of middle age whose sexual discourse is bound up with gambling and haute cuisine metaphors, are pursuing the young and naive Albertinette. Meanwhile, the prince and his wife are persuaded by the newly arrived Count Hufnagel to give a ball during which the costume of the future will be awarded a prize. The arbitrator is Maestro Fior (the Italian for flower, but also an allusion to Dior), who prophesies that fashion is the ultimate form offered to mankind, proclaiming that "fashion is history." In the background are absurd courtiers repeating nonsense phrases ("Lord Blotton's chairs"—a Pickwickian joke), while a crowd of lackeys chatter in slang and literally lick the boots of their masters. The ball, as in *Die Fledermaus* and *Arabella*, forms the substance of Act 2. Nothing, however, works as planned: Albertinette, promoted model, falls asleep in her toilette, dreaming aloud about nudity and of the pickpocket who caressed her breasts in the previous act; Count Hufnagel turns out to be Joseph, a former servant of the prince fired for insubordination and turned socialist agitator. When the costumes are revealed, the general wears a Nazi uniform and the marchioness that of a female guard of a concentration camp—the costumes of the future—while the lackeys, pickpockets, and revolutionaries take over. Act 3, set in the ruins of the chateau, is a sort of post-revolutionary nightmare, dominated by the "wooden tongue" of Communist rhetoric. But we are in an operetta and everything, as in Beaumarchais, must end in song: from the coffin brought on stage emerges the naked Albertinette, whose apparition (a new, sexual form of subversion?) leads to a choral finale in praise of youth and love.

While music, in keeping with the rules of the genre, plays an essential, indeed indispensable role in *Operetta*, Gombrowicz had

FROM *Operetta*

PRINCESS.
Master, all our hope lies in you. The master, if you please, will renovate our fashions! The master will bring men's and women's fashions up to date!

FIOR (musing).
Renovate
Men and women's fashions?...

GROUP OF GENTLEMEN.
Oh yes, oh yes, oh yes!

FIOR.
It's very well to say!
It's very well to say: create a new style!
Invent a new fashion! But what sort of new fashion?
Fashion... Fashion cannot march contrary to the times...
Fashion is time. Fashion is history!
Am I mistaken when I say
That fashion is history?

PRINCE.
It's history!

BANKER.
Fashion is history!

GENERAL.
Yes, it's history!

HUFNAGEL.
History!

PRINCESS (to the PRINCE).
Is fashion really history?

PRINCE.
Yes, fashion is history!

GROUP OF GENTLEMEN (lifting up their arms).
Fashion... is... history!
(Silence)

FIOR.
History...
I am Fior! A master am I! Master Fior!
To furnish modern man with a brand-new look?
Oh, for the masters of old it was easy to invent!
But how difficult it is today...
What will come in five, ten, fifteen years?
What will the future bring?
How time races by...
Oh, how troubled I am by an age I can't divine!
In the matrix of the present is the future contained...
O form inscrutable!
Russia... England... Maritime policy...
Delcassé...
The Balkans... Socialism... The Kronprinz...
Where to? In what direction? Towards what goal? What sort of trouser leg should I propose when I don't even know whether ten years from now trousers will be worn? Perhaps the clothes of the future will be made of feathers or metal rings... The future... The future is a dark chasm, an enigma.
History is without a face!

From *Operetta*, translated by Louis Iribarne. London: Calder and Boyars, 1971.

From Jacques Rosner's production of *Opérette* at the Théâtre national populaire at the Palais de Chaillot, 1970.

no particular composer in mind. Productions of the work have typically commissioned ad hoc music. At the time of Gombrowicz's death, it was being rehearsed by the Théâtre national populaire in Paris, where the premiere took place shortly afterwards in a production by Jacques Rosner, with music by Karel Trow, while the Italian premiere took place at the Teatro Stabile in Aquila in November 1969.

In 1965, Gombrowicz was proposed for the Prix international de littérature (formerly Formentor Prize) but was bypassed in favor of Saul Bellow, chiefly because of the opposition of Mary McCarthy, who chaired the panel of judges (thereby earning vengeful comments in the *Diary*). Gombrowicz was awarded the Prize for *Cosmos* in May 1967. This distinction, then considered the most important after the Nobel Prize, increased his fame in Western Europe, while it freed him finally from financial worries. (Gombrowicz's name started being mentioned as a candidate for the Nobel, for which he was rumored to be the favorite in the year of his death.)

In the wake of this major development, the Parisian publisher Pierre Belfond approached the young French writer and editor Dominique de Roux (1935–77) in June 1967 to prepare a volume based on conversations with Gombrowicz. An enthusiastic admirer of Gombrowicz's oeuvre, de Roux became, along with Jelenski, one of its most ardent propagators in France. He paid several visits to Vence to prepare the book. Gombrowicz, how-

Gombrowicz and Dominique de Roux on the balcony of Gombrowicz's bedroom at the Villa Alexandrine, Vence, in May–June 1967. Photo: Leprince

ever, not satisfied with the form of the spoken interview, decided to write the entire book himself in Polish. Characteristically, as the manuscript reveals, he retained the form of the conversation, writing out both the interviewer's questions and his answers, an approach that recalls the free use he made of the form of the intimate journal in the *Diary* he was still contributing to *Kultura* on a monthly basis. Along with the *Diary*, and with the *Polish memories* he had written at the end of his Argentinian period, the *Entretiens* constitute a rich autobiographical source, especially on the early years of his life, beginning with a portrait of his parents. They also contain invaluable exegeses of all his major works, from the stories of *Memories of the time of immaturity* to *Operetta*.

The *Entretiens avec Dominique de Roux* first came out in December 1968 in a French translation by Koukou Chanska and François Marié, revised by Gombrowicz. The original Polish was published by Kultura the following year.

Witold and Rita Gombrowicz with Maria Paczowska at the Hôtel Saint-Martin, Vence, 1967. Photo: Bohdan Paczowski

New friendships were formed during the Vence years. In January 1965, Gombrowicz met the architect Bohdan Paczowski and his wife Maria, a novelist. They became close friends, entertaining Gombrowicz the following summer in Chiavari, the small port on the Ligurian coast, near Genoa, where they lived. Paczowski has left some of the best photographs of Gombrowicz, several of which illustrate this catalogue. Also in January 1965, Gombrowicz was visited by Slawomir Mrozek (born in 1930), whose play *Tango*, produced the year before, had made him the leading Polish playwright of the new generation. Other visitors included the Polish painter Jozef Jarema, then living on the Riviera; the graphic artist Jan Lenica; the French philosopher Jean Wahl, whom Gombrowicz had met at Royaumont; from Latin America, the Cuban writer Severo Sarduy, who eventually settled in France, and Ernesto Sábato; and Czeslaw Milosz, who spent a month in Vence in May 1967. In March 1968, Jean Dubuffet, who owned a villa in Vence, began a lively correspondence with Gombrowicz, in which the French artist and the Polish writer debated their views on painting.

Gombrowicz with the Polish painter Jozef Jarema, Czeslaw Milosz, and Gombrowicz's English translator Alastair Hamilton, Vence, May 1967. Photo: Oswald Malura

If marked by many happy moments, Gombrowicz's Vence years were also spent in a permanent state of ill health. Human suffering, a theme present in many passages of his work, inspired a long meditation on the first part of Dante's *Divine Comedy* (his marked up copy of the French Garnier edition is preserved in the Beinecke Library) in which he questioned the Italian poet's acquiescence to the idea of eternal punishment. Published in

Witold and Rita Gombrowicz during his philosophy course, Vence, May–June 1969.
Photo: Hanne Garthe

Kultura in 1966 as part of the *Diary*, this essay was issued separately in French two years later in a collection edited by de Roux. It provoked an outraged reaction from Giuseppe Ungaretti and, according to Gombrowicz, a protest from the cultural services of the Italian embassy in Paris.

After the completion of the *Entretiens*, de Roux offered to devote to Gombrowicz a volume in the series he edited under the imprint Cahier de l'Herne. Gombrowicz enthusiastically agreed, while insisting that the tone be different from the previous Cahier devoted to Borges, which he found too adulatory. He set to work himself, assisting de Roux in preparing the table of contents and soliciting contributions. He himself contributed reminiscences of his dialogue with Bruno Schulz and a chapter (written in the third person) on "Gombrowicz et les Polonais," in which he surveyed his difficult relationship with his compatriots at home and in the emigration circles, notably his "enemies in London." This chapter was eventually completed by Olga Scherer.

On 18 November 1968, Gombrowicz suffered a heart attack, from which he took several weeks to recover. On 28 December, he and Rita Labrosse were married; by special dispensation, the ceremony took place in their apartment. At the end of March 1969, because of the lack of an elevator, they left the Villa Alexandrine and moved to a small flat at the Val-Clair, outside Vence. Despite his increasingly weak condition, Gombrowicz let himself be persuaded by de Roux to dictate to him and Rita a series of lectures on philosophy. These sessions took place in the Gombrowiczes' new home between 27 April and 25 May. Three were devoted to

Kant, the fourth and fifth to Schopenhauer, the sixth to Hegel and Kierkegaard, and the remaining ones to existentialism (Husserl, Heidegger, Sartre) and Marxism. The last session, on structuralism, was interrupted owing to Gombrowicz's ill health. Fragments of this course were published for the first time in the posthumous Cahier de l'Herne and the full text appeared in 1995 under the title *Cours de philosophie en six heures et quart.*

Also in May, Gombrowicz was interviewed at length by the French television literary journalist Michel Polac for a program in his series Bibliothèque de Poche. This document, the only such interview of Gombrowicz in existence, is an invaluable record of his lucid, opinionated, witty conversation.

Gombrowicz died in Vence on 24 July 1969 of heart failure connected with his respiratory problems.

From the exhibition:

Piotr Rawicz. "Vitold Gombrowicz à Paris." From *Le Monde* for 18 May 1963.

"Événements sur la goélette Banbury." In *Preuves*, nos. 147 and 148 (May–June 1963).

Jorge Lavelli. Letter to Witold Gombrowicz, 30 June 1963.

Jorge Di Paola Levin. *Hernán: poema dramático en cinco cuadros. Carta-prólogo de Witold Gombrowicz.* La Plata: Ediciones del Cuadrante, 1963. From the library of Witold Gombrowicz.

Mauricio Kagel. Letter to Witold Gombrowicz, 8 December 1963.

Diary for 1964, manuscript, two versions.

Kosmos. Opening page of the first version, typescript, corrected [ca. 1961] and corrected proofs, ca. 1966.

Photograph of Royaumont.

Ingmar Bergman. Letter to Witold Gombrowicz, 2 November 1964.

Photograph of the Villa Alexandrine in Vence.

Slawomir Mrozek. *Utwory sceniczne.* Cracow: Wydawnictwo literackie, 1963. Inscribed to Gombrowicz by the author.

Operetka. Manuscript of the final version, ca. 1965.

Photograph from Jacques Rosner's production of *Opérette* at the Théâtre national populaire at the Palais de Chaillot, 1970.

Adolf Rudnicki. *Weiss wpada do morza: niebieskie kartki.* Warsaw: Panstwowy Instytut Wydawniczy, 1965. Inscribed to Gombrowicz by the author.

Ernesto Sabato. *Alejandra, roman.* Traduit de l'argentin [sic] par Jean-Jacques Villard. Avant-propos de Witold Gombrowicz. Paris: Éditions du Seuil, 1967. Inscribed to Gombrowicz by the translator.

Piers Paul Read. Letter to Witold Gombrowicz, 31 December 1966.

Alf Sjöberg. Letter to Witold Gombrowicz, 12 December 1966.

Program of Alf Sjöberg production of *Yvonne, prinsessa av Bourgogne*, at the Dramatiska Teatern (Stockholm, Sweden), 1966.

Program of Alf Sjöberg production of *The marriage* at the Dramatiska Teatern (Stockholm, Sweden), 1966.

Photograph from the Sjöberg production of *The marriage*.

Dante. *La Divine Comédie.* Traduction, préface, notes et commentaires, par Henri Longnon. Paris: Garnier Frères, 1962. Gombrowicz's copy.

Photograph of Gombrowicz at his desk at the Villa Alexandrine in Vence.

Gombrowicz and Dominique de Roux on the balcony of Gombrowicz's bedroom at the Villa Alexandrine, Vence, in May–June 1967.

Entretiens avec Dominique de Roux (Testament). Manuscript, 1967–68.

Photograph of Gombrowicz with Jozef Jarema, Czeslaw Milosz, and Alastair Hamilton, Vence, May 1967.

Photograph of Witold and Rita Gombrowicz with Maria Paczowska at the Hôtel Saint-Martin, Vence, 1967.

Photograph of Witold and Rita Gombrowicz with their dog Psina in their Citroën 2-CV, Vence, 1967.

Jaime Salinas. Letter to Witold Gombrowicz, 8 May 1967.

Yvonne, princesse de Bourgogne [poster]. Compagnie Bernard Fontaine. Nice: Centre culturel méditerranéen, 1967.

Jean Dubuffet. Letter to Witold Gombrowicz, 7 March 1968.

Artur Sandauer. Letter to Witold Gombrowicz, 8 August 1968.

Cosmos. Tradução de Luiza Neto Jorge. Lisbon: Editora Ulisseia, 1966.

Pornografia: a novel. Translated by Alastair Hamilton. London: Calder and Boyars, 1966. From the library of Witold Gombrowicz.

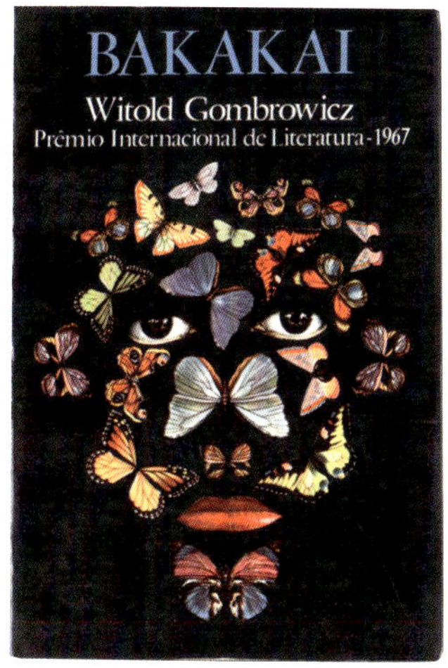

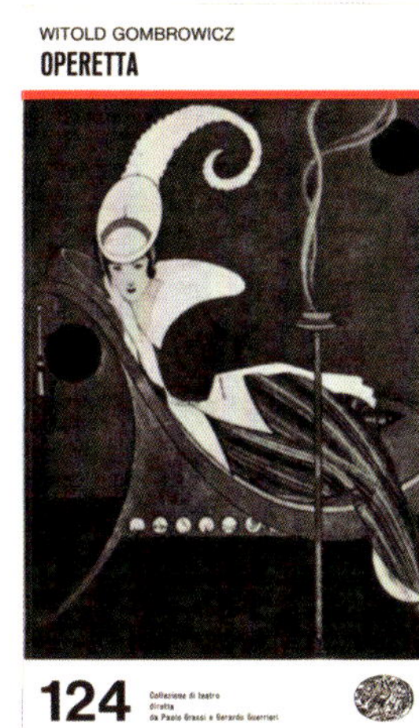

La seducción. Barcelona: Editorial Seix Barral, 1968. From the library of Witold Gombrowicz.

Bakakai. Rio de Janeiro: Editôra Expressão e Cultura, 1968. From the library of Witold Gombrowicz.

Operetta. Turin: Giulio Einaudi editore, 1968. From the library of Witold Gombrowicz.

The marriage. Translated by Louis Iribane. London: Calder and Boyars, 1969. From the library of Witold Gombrowicz.

Pornografia. Milan: Bompiani, 1962 (I più famosi libri moderni, no. 257). From the library of Witold Gombrowicz.

Photograph of Ernst Schröder's production of *The marriage* in Berlin, 1968.

Drafts of dedications to General de Gaulle, 1969.

"Stroke and marriage." Manuscript fragment from the *Diary* for 1969.

Manuscript notes for the Cahier de l'Herne [1969].

Rita Gombrowicz. Autograph notebook recording Gombrowicz's philosophical course, May–June 1969.

Photograph of Witold and Rita Gombrowicz during his philosophy course, Vence, May–June 1969.

Telegrams to Rita Gombrowicz from Kultura, Paris; Théâtre national populaire, Paris; Jerzy Andrzejewski; Czeslaw Milosz, July 1969.

Gombrowicz. Paris: L'Herne, 1971.

SELECTED BIBLIOGRAPHY

I. *Works by Gombrowicz in English*

1. Autobiographical

Diary (1953–1956). General editor: Jan Kott. Translated by Lillian Vallee. Preface by Wojciech Karpinski. Postface by Jan Kott. Evanston: Northwestern University Press; London: Quartet Press, 1988.

Diary (1957–1961). General editor: Jan Kott. Translated by Lillian Vallee. Postface by the translator. Evanston: Northwestern University Press; London: Quartet Press, 1989.

Diary (1957–1968). General editor: Jan Kott. Translated by Lillian Vallee. Postface by the translator. Evanston: Northwestern University Press; London: Quartet Press, 1993. This edition does not include the diary of 1969. *The three volumes were reissued in a slipcase, 1994.*

A kind of testament. Translated [from the French] by Alastair Hamilton. Preface by Maurice Nadeau. London: Calder and Boyars, 1973. Though adapted from the French text, the English edition does not retain the form of an interview.

Polish memories. Translated by Bill Johnston. New Haven: Yale University Press, 2004.

"Argentine peregrinations" is not available in English but can be read in French (*Pérégrinations argentines*, translated by Allan Kosko, Paris: Christian Bourgois, 1984) or in Spanish (*Peregrinaciones argentinas*, translated by Sergio Pitol, Buenos Aires: Hidalgo, 2001).

2. Fiction

Bacacay. Translated by Bill Johnston. New York: Archipelago Press, 2004.

Cosmos. Translated [from the French and the German] by Eric Mosbacher. London: MacGibbon & Kee, 1967. Published in the U. S. by The Grove Press, New York, 1967; reissued in a single volume with *Ferdydurke* and *Pornografia*, 1978; reissued in a single volume with *Pornografia*, 1985. A new translation from the Polish by Danuta Borchardt is in preparation, to be published by Yale University Press.

Ferdydurke. Translated [from the French] by Eric Mosbacher. London: MacGibbon & Kee, 1961. Published in the U. S. by Harcourt Brace, New York, 1961; reissued by The Grove Press, New York, 1965 (reissued in one volume with *Cosmos* and *Pornografia*, 1978). Paperback edition, Penguin, London, 1989.

Ferdydurke. Translated by Danuta Borchardt. Preface by Susan Sontag. New Haven and London: Yale University Press, 2000.

Pornografia. Translated [from the French] by Alastair Hamilton. London; Calder and Boyars, 1966. Reprinted in 1994. Published in the U.S. by The Grove Press, New York, 1966 (reissued in one volume with *Ferdydurke* and *Cosmos*, 1978). Available in paperback from Penguin, London, 1991, and in a single volume with *Cosmos*, The Grove Press, 1985.

Possessed, or The secret of Myslotch. Translated [from the French] by J. A. Underwood. London and Boston: Marion Boyars, 1980. Reprinted in 1988 and 1998.

Trans-Atlantyk. Translated by Carolyn French and Nina Karsov. Preface by Stanislaw Baranczak. New Haven and London: Yale University Press, 1994.

3. Theater

[*Historia*] *History (an operetta).* Translated by Allen Kuharski and Dariusz Bukowski. Presentation by Allen Kuharski. In *Periphery*, 1 (1995), 56–69.

[*Iwona*] *Princess Ivona.* Translated by Krystyna Griffith-Jones and Catherine Robbins. London: Calder and Boyars, 1969. Published in the U. S. as *Ivona, princess of Burgundia* by The Grove Press, New York, 1970.

[*Operetka*] *Operetta.* Translated by Louis Iribarne. London: Calder and Boyars, 1971. Published in the U. S. by The Grove Press, New York, 1971.

[*Slub*] *The marriage.* Translated by Louis Iribarne. New York: The Grove Press, 1969. Published in the U. K. by Calder and Boyars, 1970.

Three plays: Princess Ivona; The marriage; Operetta. Introductory essay by Jerzy Peterkiewicz. Translated by Krystyna Griffith-Jones, Catherine Robbins, and Louis Iribarne. London and New York: Marion Boyars, 1998.

4. Varia

A guide to philosophy in six hours. To be published by Yale University Press in 2004.

II. *Further reading*

1. General and biographical

Giedroyc, Jerzy, and Witold Gombrowicz. *Correspondance 1950–1969.* Translated and edited by Jean-Claude Famulicki. Paris: Fayard, 2004. An important correspondence between Gombrowicz and his principal editor and publisher. The only other selections of letters in languages other than Polish are in the Cahier de l'Herne (the exchange with Dubuffet was also issued in book form) and *Gombrowicz vingt ans après.* An unauthorized edition of the correspondence between Gombrowicz and Juan Carlos Gómez was published in Argentina.

Gombrowicz, Rita. *Gombrowicz en Argentine: témoignages et documents 1939–1963.* Préface de Constantin Jelenski. Paris: Denoël, 1984. Contributors include Mariano Betelú, Jorge Luis Borges, Jorge Di Paola, Manuel Gálvez, Juan Carlos Gómez, Carlos Mastronardi, Jacobo Muchnik, Adolfo de Obieta, Silvina Ocampo, Virgilio Piñera, Roger Plá, Humberto Rodriguez Tomeu, Alejandro Rússovich, Maria Swieczewska, among others. With a chronology and a bibliography.

Gombrowicz, Rita. *Gombrowicz en Europe: témoignages et documents 1963–1969.* Paris: Denoël, 1988. Includes contributions from Constantin Jelenski, Jerzy Giedroyc, Zofia and Zygmunt Hertz, Józef Czapski, Gustaw Herling-Grudzinski, Czeslaw Milosz, François Bondy, Maurice Nadeau, Marc Pierret, Hector Bianciotti, Jorge Lavelli, Diego Masson, Olivier Lebeault, Juliette Brac, Alexis Nitzer, Fernand Berset, Ingeborg Bachman, Günter Grass, Uwe Johnson, Walter Höllerer, Helmut Jaesrich, Walter Hasenclever, Michel Butor,

Piers Paul Read, Eva Bechman, Otto Schilly, Klaus Völker, Frédéric Benrath, Otto Mertens, Waltraut Kurpiers, Tadeusz Kulik, Susanna Fels, Alain and Isabelle Crespelle, Bernard Guiéry, Eddy Trèves, Georges Lapassade, Jean Kalman, Martine Millon, Guy de Bosschère, Janusz Odrowaz-Pienazek, Georges and Véronique Charaire, Edgar Reichmann, Elisabeth Orel, and a personal memoir by Rita Gombrowicz. The "Documents" section includes translations of letters by Gombrowicz; the bibliography is limited to articles on Gombrowicz in French.

Gombrowicz, Witold. *Moi et mon double.* Paris: Gallimard, Quarto, 1996. Edited by Françoise Cibiel in collaboration with Jean-Louis Panné, Brigitte de la Broise, Guénola de Metz, and Antoine Jacottet. Contains the entirety of Gombrowicz's fiction in one volume, with a detailed chronology and additional documents.

Gombrowicz, vingt ans après. Suivi de Correspondances et Une jeunesse. Edited by Manuel Carcassonne, Christophe Guias, Malgorzata Smorag. Paris: Christian Bourgois, 1989. Published to mark the twentieth anniversary of Gombrowicz's death, this useful volume contains contributions by François Bondy, Jorge Lavelli, and Philippe Sollers, among others; Gombrowicz's correspondences with Józef Wittlin, presented by Renata Gorzynska; with Constantin Jelenski, presented by Wojciech Karpinski; and with Dominique de Roux, presented by Pierre-Guillaume de Roux; and testimonies by members of the Gombrowicz family.

Roux, Dominique de, and Constantin Jelenski, editors. *Gombrowicz.* Paris: L'Herne, 1971. Contains texts by and contributions from Pierre Babin, Renato Barilli, Jean-Marie Benoist, Michel Bernard, Pawel Beylin, François Bondy, Kazimierz Brandys, Tadeusz Breza, David Brodsky, Zofia Chadzynska, Jerzy Cieniewicz, E. M. Cioran, André Coyné, Józef Czapski, Ariel Denis, Jean Dubuffet, Michel Foucault, Matthew Galey, Étienne Gilson, Günter Grass, Lars Gustafsson, Alastair Hamilton, Claude Jannoud, Pierre-Benoît Jeannin, Uwe Johnson, René Julliard, Andrzej Kijowski, Jan Kott, Jerzy Kosinski, Georges Lapassade, Jorge Lavelli, Georges Lisowski, Zdravko Malic, Carlos Mastronardi, Czeslaw Milosz, Slawomir Mrozek, Napoléon Murat, Mario Oks, Eric Pardineille, Jerzy Peterkiewicz, Marc Pierret, Konstanty Puzyna, S.W. de Rachewiltz, Édouard Roditi, Piero Sanavio, Artur Sandauer, Jean-Paul Sartre, Olga Scherer, Bruno Schulz, Georges Sédir, Jerzy Szymkowicz-Gombrowicz, Giuseppe Ungaretti, Jean-Noël Vuarnet, Józef Wittlin, and Pawel Zdziechowski. Gombrowicz himself contributed the chronology of his life (an unreliable, if invaluable document, which has been reprinted, mistakes included, in *Testament*, the English version of *Entretiens avec Dominique de Roux*) and the essay "Gombrowicz et les Polonais."

2. Interpretive

Dedieu, Jean-Claude. *Witold Gombrowicz.* Paris: Marval, 1993. A short essay, illustrated with Gombrowicz-inspired photographs by Magdi Senadji.

Georgin, Rosine. *Gombrowicz.* Lausanne: L'âge d'homme, 1977. Revised edition, Paris: Cistre, 1987. Generally considered one of the best books on Gombrowicz in languages other than Polish.

Karpinski, Wojciech. *Ces livres de grand chemin,* tr. by Elisabeth Destrée-Van Wilder. Montricher (Switzerland): Noir sur blanc,

1992. French translation of *Ksiazki zbójeckie* (London: Polonia, 1988). Contains two chapters on Gombrowicz.

Kundera, Milan. *Testaments betrayed: an essay in nine parts.* Translated from the French by Nina Ascher. New York: HarperCollins, 1995. Contains an appraisal of *Ferdydurke* p. 250–52 by one of Gombrowicz's most fervent contemporary champions. There are also a few references to Gombrowicz in Kundera's *The art of the novel*, translated from the French by Nina Ascher, New York: The Grove Press, 1988.

Milosz, Czeslaw. *The history of Polish literature.* New York: Macmillan, 1969. Revised edition, Berkeley, California: The University of California Press, 1983. Contains several pages on Gombrowicz.

Milosz, Czeslaw. *The land of Ulro.* Translated by Louis Iribarne. New York: Farrar, Straus, Giroux, 1984. The book is devoted in part to Gombrowicz.

Nadeau, Maurice. *Grâces leur soient rendues.* Paris: Albin Michel, 1990. A memoir by the critic and publisher and an early champion of Gombrowicz in France.

Peiron, Johanna. *Gombrowicz, écrivain et stratège: un auteur "excentrique" face à la France.* Paris: L'Harmattan, 2002.

Proguidis, Lakis. *Un écrivain malgré la critique: essai sur l'oeuvre de Witold Gombrowicz.* Paris: Gallimard, 1989.

Roux, Dominique de. *Gombrowicz.* Paris: Christian Bourgois, 1971, reprinted 1978. This highly readable essay (which includes the account of an interview with Vladimir Nabokov) is not to be confused with the Cahier de l'Herne de Roux edited in 1971 on Gombrowicz.

Salgas, Jean-Pierre. *Witold Gombrowicz, ou l'athéisme généralisé.* Paris; Seuil, 2000 (Collection Les contemporains).

Thompson, Ewa M. *Witold Gombrowicz.* Boston: Twayne Publishers, 1979. The first general study of Gombrowicz published in English. Includes a biographical introduction, analyses of the short stories, plays, novels, *Diary*, and a bibliography.

Volle, Jacques. *Gombrowicz, bourreau, martyr.* Paris: Christian Bourgois, 1972.

Ziarek, Ewa Plonowska, editor. *Gombrowicz's grimaces: modernism, gender, nationality.* Albany: State University of New York Press, 1998. A collection of essays by American and European scholars; includes a short bibliography.